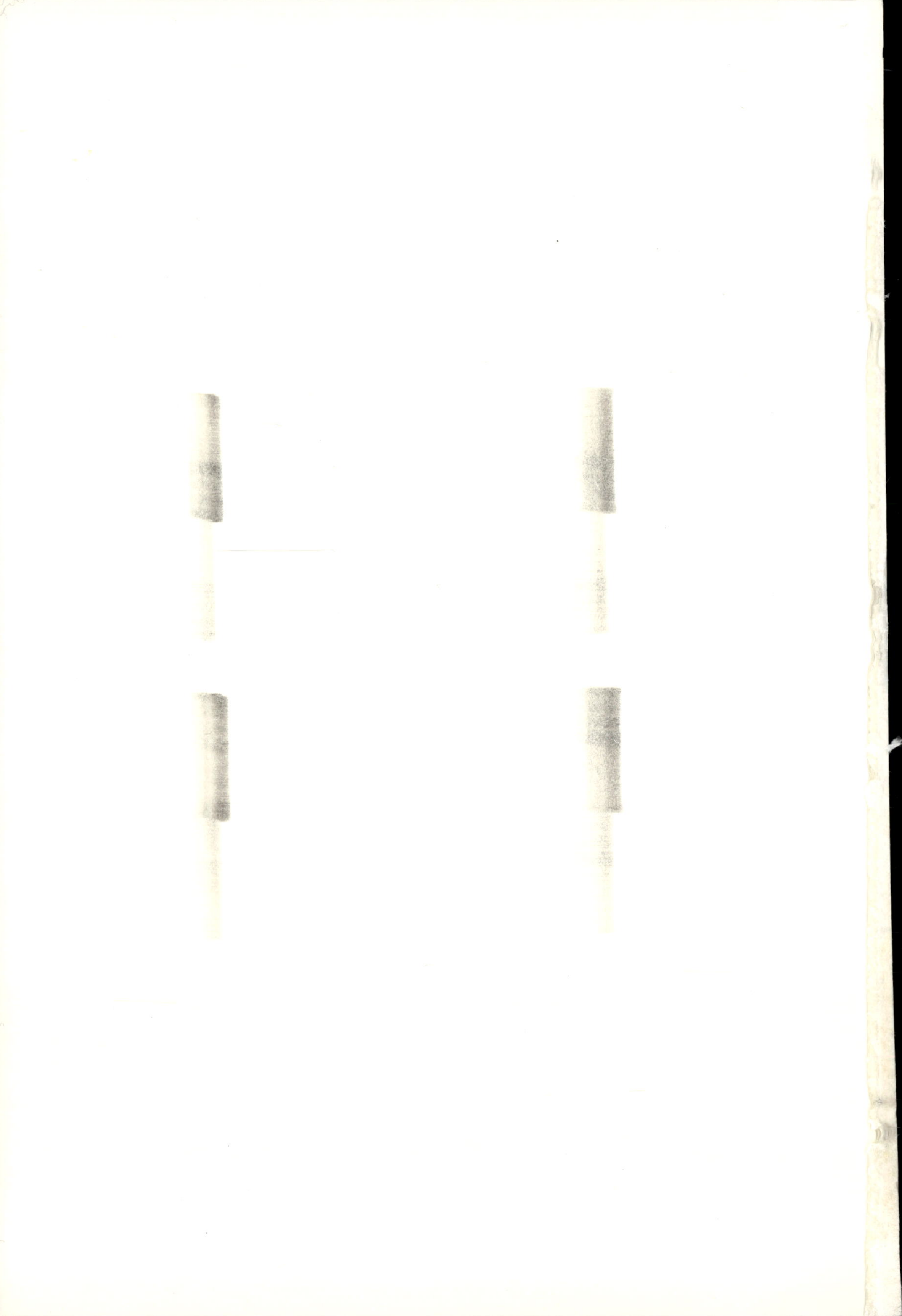

California Fever Dream
A Memoir

Judy Juanita

WILLOW BOOKS, a Division of Aquarius Press
Detroit, MI

California Fever Dream
A Memoir

Copyright © 2026 by Judy Juanita

Cover art: Harper Communications Group

ISBN 979-8-21893564-1
LCCN 2026936455

Willow Books, a Division of Aquarius Press
www.WillowLit.net

Printed in the United States of America

Contents

Judith Hart

Judy Juanita

JUDITH HART

THE CALIFORNIA FEVER DREAM

Al Young was a poet, novelist, essayist, a gentleman and a scholar, and a mentor to me and many others. His tribes gathered to celebrate his life in June, 2023, a unique assemblage of intellectuals, poets and writers, erstwhile Beats, admirers of the gentle, affable king who was the Poet Laureate of California from 2005 to 2008, and Ishmael Reed, his great friend and another of my mentors, who gave, in essence the keynote address. Al left this world April 17, 2021, at 81 (COVID delayed his memorial). His loving son Michael, who nursed him through his final illness, nailed the quintessential quality that drove his father and others to the golden state. *A California fever dream* is how Michael memorialized his father's great spirit. That fever drew him to California. My parents came in their *fever dream* from Oklahoma during WWII.

I was born in Berkeley (1946) into a world where my parents owned the only black cab company in the Eastbay. A world where my uncle had a big rooming house that welcomed family from Oklahoma in chain migration. A world where relatives saved change in Mason jars to finance neat bungalows in Berkeley and Oakland. A world where my mother's friend ran her own 5-and-dime on Alcatraz Ave. A world where blacks couldn't use the segregated pool in the Berkeley Y except one night a week. A world where blacks congregated in churches, fraternal organizations, union groups, and social clubs that harked back to the Okie past.. The Langston Club, The Muskogee Club, The Guthrie Club. A world that became extinct as my parents' generation died. Honoring Al's illustrious life drove me to look at becoming a poet, novelist, essayist, playwright, and mentor, as my own *fever dream.*

A FAMILY STORY

The story of my grandfather, Albert H. Hart Sr., is a self-published book that my Aunt Florence, his sister whom I am said to resemble, composed and gave to family. There have been many daydreams throughout my family about what to do with all the millions Papa Hart, an Oklahoma oil scout and oilman, made for the white business partners that ripped him off. I've been busy writing, teaching and studying other people's lives—I love biographies and history. But, around the time I finished my first novel, I realized my defensiveness and assiduous avoidance had kept me from my own family saga.

PAPA HART

Family storytellers say Papa Hart was keen on pretty Creek and Cherokee girls and beat a path to their grounds. While in pursuit, he came to know the territory. It was the 1910s and 1920s; the oil boom in Oklahoma had commenced in 1897. Papa Hart knew the plain, the brush, the wilderness as well as anyone. Oil speculators got hold of him and began paying him to scout out locations for oil wells. Soon, young Albert got rich, married a beautiful Creek girl named Mary with whom he had three children, Irma Jean, Marion and Albert (my dad). Meanwhile the oil speculators were in cahoots with the local bank. But everybody was making tons of money and living high on the hog.

Then the speculators got caught, charged and convicted of bank fraud and forgery, and sent to prison. Before they left, they signed over the deeds to the property to young Hart. When they got out of prison, a few years hence, they came looking for Hart. When he refused to sign over the deeds, they took him out on the plains and beat the living daylights out of him. They took the deeds and left him to die. He didn't die but his prodigious brain power was gone. The rest of the family left him in Oklahoma and migrated to California. Sunny California in the 1930s was the next era for my family. When I first read *Grapes of Wrath* by John Steinbeck, I didn't even know family history well enough to see the book's parallel to my life. I was that ignorant-- busy getting away from my family and what I perceived as their dominance and belittling of me. It has taken a lifetime to turn around and appreciate my rich family history.

My mother was not Indian ["I'm a pure Negro"] but wanted my father to share our Indian heritage with us when we were kids. Dad said it would just confuse us. Same rationale for not telling us about his father, the oil millionaire. So we heard rumors about this Indian business through the larger family, mostly negative innuendos, like "That's why you can't hold your liquor; that's the Indian in you." My siblings and I were made fun of because my skin coloring was said to be Indian-like but my hair nappy, while my brother and sister were darker-skinned with shiny, blacker, straighter hair. It wasn't until the black pride movement of the 1960s/70s and the subsequent ethnic pride movements that the rumors came out in the open.

GOOD, HONEST, TRIBAL ANCESTRY

Aunt Irma Jean, dad's sister, lived with us for a few weeks when I was a kid. Her seven kids and the four of us, Dad, Mom and Aunt Irma Jean, lived in our three-bedroom house in East Oakland until they found a house nearby. It was big fun for the kids; it was like having a new best friend to walk to school with, a three month slumber party. Aunt Irma Jean, who got a PhD. in English and taught all over the world, was outspoken about Papa Hart and Mama Hart's Indian heritages all along, and about a lot else too. Her daughter Carol,my age, grew up and married Jack Forbes of the Lenape/Powhatan tribes [the late Jack D. Forbes, Ph.D., founder/ chair of Native American Studies, UC Davis]. Cousin Jack conducted immense research into our family along with being an eminent Native American scholar. He said, "If we have African blood we should be proud of it; it is good, honest, tribal ancestry." (Attan-Akamik Newsletter, 1974). His last book, published just after he died in 2011, *Africans and Native Americans: the language of race and the evolution of Red-Black peoples*, tackled the same issue various family had side-eyed and suppressed throughout my childhood, the intersection of Native Americans and African Americans.

THE AMERICAN DREAM

My dad was born in 1916 in an all-black town, Beggs, Oklahoma, nearly a decade after Oklahoma became a state, and 27 years after the great Land Run of 1889. Belongingness, prosperity, the roads to success and individual achievement were my dad's issues, his dad's issues, and they're mine. The American dream. On the day after Pearl Harbor, my father, Albert H. Hart II, who had been working as a machinist at Treasure Island, enrolled in the Army. He was sent to Tuskegee Army Air Field, Alabama, where a special unit of Negro soldiers was being trained for the Army Air Force. They were the Tuskegee Airmen.

Dad called himself a "race man"—a black man who would not stand to be treated as a "nigger" but instead stood up to the white man. A race man was aware of the history of brutality and oppression against members of his race. He just would not go along to get along. My dad told me that the soldiers in Tuskegee went into town on their day off and protested the white theater seating, the Jim Crow laws in the town. For that, they were severely disciplined, but they weren't about to go overseas and give their lives when they couldn't even have basic rights here.

Dad was in the 332nd Fighter Group and served in Italy. Dad's best friend was a pilot while Dad was ground crew. In Italy, on their first weekend there, Dad's friend flew out on a training mission. His plane hit the face of a mountain and he was killed instantly. My father, who by then was married to my mother, had a picture she'd sent him of her and his new son (my big brother Skip). He took it into the Italian town to be framed, but because of wartime there was a lack of glass for framing. Instead, the framer ended up using pieces of the windshield from the plane that crashed to make an impromptu frame.

The picture still exists today and periodically disappears. I call the people who spirit away these valued family treasures "picture thieves"—and have to admit that, from time to time, I have been a picture thief. But because of technology, I now make copies for all to have.

HOW BLACK BECAME BEAUTIFUL

How black became beautiful with a capital "B" is the story of the 1960s for me. Before that era which began in the 50s, the words "Negro" and "colored" were accepted ways black people self-referenced. To be called black was an insult of the highest order alongside nigger; it was not only a slur against skin tone, but a sensitized demarcation of destiny, marital prospects, choice of neighborhood, friends, habits, goals, and lifelong prospects. I overheard my dad, at one point a mailman, refer to a section of Oakland around Lake Merritt as 'nigger Piedmont" in conversation with his friends. Piedmont is the exclusive, mostly white town entirely inside Oakland, absolutely and rigidly red-lined before the 1960s. Realtors enforced the geographic prohibition of blacks, even those who could afford it. Oakland Municipal Court Judge Lionel Wilson, who would become Oakland's first black mayor, was one of the fabled residents of Mandana Blvd., the main artery and success meter for black attorneys, doctors, and other professionals. In that context the term 'nigger Piedmont" was not a slur. It was a statement of boundary, i.e. this is where black people with means live in Oakland. My younger sister, who was pretty much wild and out there from childhood, was suspended from school when she called one of her colored teachers a "black nigger" –doubly transgressive. She got whipped at home for using those two lethal words. So, then, how did black capitalize itself and turn into a praiseworthy term? One way and one way only. Black women. One by one, we stopped straightening their hair and began seeing ourselves anew in the mirror of our daily lives. In my novel Virgin Soul, set in the 1960s, its young protagonist Geniece encounters new attitudes toward her marginalized black skin and features at The Black House, a real place in San Francisco that I visited often when I was a junior at SF State. Here is the novelized version of my own transformation:

Fatimah stood in the kitchen, smiling at me as if she had been waiting for me all night. I touched my hair. It felt wiry and woolly. She smiled again.

"You are a queen. Beautiful," she said. I didn't know what to say. Beautiful. What kind of word was that to be connected with me? I had been called cute and dark, sexy and dark, long-legged and dark.
Beautiful?

"You've never been called that, have you? A queen?" she asked, her voice soft and rich.

"No, never," I said. Napoleon nose had been one of my nicknames from the cousins. I had a small waist and pretty feet, my one physically perfect feature. Men had singled out parts, as if the whole was worth very little but the parts could be worth something at auction. I never believed men who said I was fine because I thought they used the word interchangeably with the thought of wanting to fuck me. The brother who had called her a Nubian came to the kitchen.

"Tightening her up?" he said.

"Harris." Fatimah's large brown eyes seemed to pour the word out to him. She had been cooking for him, I was sure. He turned to talk to someone down the hall. "Let the white kids lead a palace revolt. Let the white man be divided. Divided he falls, united we stand. When the man closes ranks is when we should be alarmed. That's when he's at his deadliest."

He turned back to me and said to Fatimah, "Lumumba, Patrice Lumumba. She's got that same steady look in her eyes. She's got a chilling thing going down in her eyes. Yeah."

My only frame of reference for anybody's Lumumba was a dark-as night boy in high school with very African features. From the South, he wore Big Ben overalls and clunky workingman's shoes, and kids called him Lumumba. He had a crush on me and my friends had made fun of me because of it. They had called me Lumumba's wife, which I had hated.

When Harris walked away, I felt free to ask Fatimah. "Am I seeing things wrong or do I just happen to see a lot of light-skinned brothers in the movement with darker-skinned sisters?" She laughed a tinkly crystal laugh. I wondered what her hair was like under her scarf.

"You picked up on that, huh? These brothers have an elevated consciousness and, yes, they're trying to prove something. Allwood is your man, right?

I shrugged. She smiled like she knew something I didn't.

"Harris, Allwood, our light-skinned men in the movement, they feel deeply about us as sisters, as beautiful black women."

"But is it overcompensation?"

"Maybe you see it as overcompensation. When you look outwardly, unless you look in a mirror, you can't see yourself. You can't see if you're skinny or fat or white or black. You see the people around you. Whatever they are, that's what you are. When you wake up in the morning, you wake up human, no age, no color, and no sex until your eye hits either a mirror or another person. Then it's instant. That's who you are—who you sleep with, who you eat with. So I think these brothers have grown to resent being categorized, put down because of their light skin. They're trying to prove who they are inside so they won't be judged by the outside."

I felt a sense of alarm. "Will they dump the dark-skinned sister once they've made their point?"

She laughed again. "Did Malcolm leave Betty?"

"Malcolm X's wife was dark-skinned?"

Fatimah got a book from a stack on the table and showed me Betty Shabazz's picture. "Brother Malcolm's overcompensation benefited us all. He became as powerful as we are. He exposed us to our power and that was his power. That's why they had to kill him."

She put the book back and walked behind me. "Let me show

you something."

With one deft movement of her hands, she twisted my hair, tighter than I had ever twisted it, into a ponytail. She pulled me up and we went to the mirror in the hall. I looked at her hands, at her long smooth fingers, with their white half-moons. They told me my mother had strong fingers with beautiful half moons. "Do you see how different you look with your hair off your face?" she asked me.

For so long, I had used my hair as my shield. To see myself in front of her as I saw myself in the morning was a shock.

"You are a beautiful woman." She turned my chin from side to side. "Look at your face, your jaw, those beautiful planes. Look at the light picking them out. You're a thousand years old. They couldn't beat the African out of you. They couldn't fuck it out."

MIGRATING, SCRIMPING AND SAVING

Leaving the south, the KKK, lynching and brutal segregation also meant leaving rural country sides, hills, mountains, vegetable gardens, fruit trees, homegrown produce, dairy and livestock. A livelihood was much harder to sustain as blacks congregated in Chicago, Harlem, Detroit, Kansas City, Los Angeles, Oakland, San Francisco, and Philadelphia. The Brotherhood of Sleeping Car Porters was essential to the migration. Blacks left on trains, often with nothing more than a box lunch cooked by a loving relative or grandma, a few dollars, and the assurance that a family friend or network of relatives from the hometown would always be available for a place to stay or a hot meal. That porter was one of the highest positions that blacks could aspire to in that era. The Bay Area was a key destination for several reasons: Berkeley and Oakland were the last stops on the Santa Fe Railroad, thus a logical destination in the migration route; and the shipyards at Treasure Island and Mare Island were primary employers hiring blacks during WWII. My Uncle Charles and Aunt Agnes owned a boarding house in Berkeley. My father's people migrated in units, boarding at Charles and Agnes' while they saved their pennies in Mason jars. They worked and saved, scrimped and moved into houses in Berkeley and East Oakland, leaving space for the next family member to come up from the South.

On mom's side, her Uncle Walter had a different reason to migrate from his hometown of Muskogee, Oklahoma. Walter fell in love with Emily, a fair-skinned African-American girl who was mistaken for white. They decided to marry. The day he did, my grandmother's employer came over to her house and told her that her brother Walter needed to get out of town immediately [as in "the next train running"] or be lynched for marrying a white woman. It didn't matter that the employer knew Emily was colored; the mob thought she was white.

Walter left town that night and resettled in Joplin, Missouri. Emily followed soon after and they remained married until her death. After she died, Walter married my Aunt Fanny, who had a little boy named Garvin Tutt. Garvin grew up and joined the Army becoming a career officer, a lieutenant colonel. We visited him and his family often when he was stationed at The Presidio in San Francisco. He and Dad traded war stories while we played with Garvin's two daughters, one of whom, Barbara, grew up to become a U.S. Congresswoman and Mayor of Oakland named Barbara Lee.

BACK TO MYSELF

Devouring biographies and immersing myself in history has fed me all my life. I pick 800 and 900 page tomes, the longer the better to lose myself in them. Sometimes I tear them into thirds and tackle the reading over a year or two. Lately, I've been gloriously entangled in *Che: A Revolutionary Life (*Jon Lee Anderson*)* and *Reformations: The Early Modern World, 1450-1650* (Carlos M.N. Eire). The struggles of the religious reformers after Martin Luther and the startling reversals in Che Guevara's revolutionary path keep leading me, like a cat chasing its tail, back to myself--and my family who have been extraordinarily present at key historical junctures.

It's taken me a long time to understand that self-disparagement is a form of humility and not a mark of low self-esteem. And likewise, when my family, full of illustrious people who've fought the good fight and died ignominiously, cuts me down to size, that it is not belittling but preparing me to be gracious in the face of the humiliation and reversals that accompany people who fight hard for what they believe.

The Three Albert Haywood Harts

Pix of my brother, Albert Haywood Hart III

Pix of my dad, Albert Haywood Hart Jr.

Pix of my grandfather, Albert Haywood Hart Sr.

A CALIFORNIA CHILDHOOD: Growing up Oakland

If trips to San Francisco were the lemon meringue on the pies that my mother fixed from scratch on Sundays, Oakland was the dark-gravied succulent roast. My siblings and I chewed on it and grew strong in a childhood centered on family, church, playing, books and school. We were the second black family on a children-filled block of identical three-bedroom stucco houses, our neighborhood a mosaic: kids from Hawaii, Mexico, the family of Mormons next door, and the family from Georgia across the street. We plotted outside sleepovers, blankets draped over poles set up in our backyards. Blackness was nothing to think about, an alien ship floating on the screen of life far away. What separated us was not race; the boys slept in one yard, the girls another.

My big brother Skippy ruled. I was two years younger. The earthquakes that rumbled and once split the driveway a foot wide were thrilling, but no more threatening than the horror movies we saw for three soda pop caps. During intermission, Skippy stood at the concession stand and turned his eyelids inside out and made the pupils disappear. When little kids turned and saw him, they screamed and ran. On Sundays we helped Skippy deliver the Oakland Tribune and the San Francisco Chronicle, my father piling us into the Ford Fairlane. Coming in from the cold to a breakfast of grits, eggs, bacon and juice was worth the newsprint-stained fingers.

GE, we bring good things to life, the ad on the television blared. Behind our house was the General Electric factory that didn't hire coloreds. A creek ran underneath it. Parents warned that it carried unspeakable things from the undertaker four blocks north. But the boys found it led to the estuary and the San Francisco Bay. My girlfriend and I decided to go by ourselves. We ironed our pedal pusher outfits, packed lunch and set out. The dried mud and briny water dirtied our sneakers. We squatted and walked single file beneath the factory. Disgusted, we couldn't turn back. Swatting all manner of bugs and creepy crawlies, we tromped through waist-high marsh for three hours to bring back our jar of guppies, our proof. I was better at going to the doll hospital with my mother in downtown Oakland. I loved tending my pink-cheeked porcelain dolls, braiding their yellow yarn hair and sewing their dresses and underpants.

Friday nights we stood and saluted the flag, singing the national anthem before my dad watched the fights on TV. My father, a Joe Louis look-alike, had served in the war as a Tuskegee Airman, 332nd squadron. I didn't realize his historic contribution until I got older. Then I only knew he loved punching along with Sugar Ray. We loved TV but hated choosing *I Love Lucy* on Mondays or *Make Room for Daddy* on Tuesdays. Reading was more important to my parents. My father, an insatiable reader, was a "race man"-a natural rebel, often leaving or getting fired jobs when he wouldn't put up with demeaning racial slurs. He developed another life at the racetrack and poker club.

My mother, also a reader, was sweet, deeply religious and superbly practical. She met Dad at Langston University in Oklahoma where he was planning to be a minister. Then he went to war. She graduated and became part of FDR's newly integrated federal civil service. When my parents married she migrated to California before he was discharged. I was born in Berkeley. While working his postal route, my father spotted our house a stone's throw from a playfield and schools. My mother saved for the down payment in a Mason jar. A fellow Oklahoman helped move us; we curled up and watched *The Jackie Gleason Show* until we fell asleep.

During the Eisenhower years, Mom jump-started our Saturday housecleaning by saying: "What if the President of the United States came to our house tomorrow!" We'd polish and dust as if Ike himself was going to visit. My father often worked the cannery near our house. From early spring until late fall the refrigerator burst with peaches, apples, nectarines, plums and apricots. On rainy days, we played for hours in our parents' bedroom, trying on Dad's big overcoats and my mother's high heels and rhinestone brooches, playing Nat King Cole LPs,

We were the first family on the block to visit Disneyland, going three summers in a row. We traveled in a trailer first to Yosemite where we bunked in the trailer, Dad in the car in case of hungry bears. We ate fish from the river fried over the cook site outside the trailer. The hungry bear showed up while Dad was sleeping. The growling awakened us; we jumped up and rocked the trailer, waking up Dad with our screaming. The bear went away but my heart wouldn't stop pounding in the night. During the day, we played with white children from families from Idaho and Nevada while the dads fished and talked at the waterfall's edge and the mothers watched us all. To get to Disneyland, we drove alongside the dusty big rigs on Route 99, close enough to see that crop dusters were bicycles with wings. When we got to the winding old Grapevine outside Los Angeles, Dad crawled around the hairpin curves. I couldn't sleep, petrified we would fall off the shoulder and never be found.

A goody-goody, I was not immune to malicious mischief. My friends and I fooled on the phone, calling boys we had crushes on and hanging up, dialing numbers at random and asking, "Is your refrigerator running?" To the few who replied, we'd say, "You better go catch it." My worst phone mischief took place at the height of the Mickey Mouse Club mania when kids dreamed of becoming a Mousketeer. Z___ was a precocious student a grade under me. Her parents showered her with lessons – piano, violin, viola, voice, tap, ballet. We considered her a big baby, but she performed at assemblies as if she was about to be discovered anytime. One afternoon, we concocted a scheme. After practicing fake voices, we dialed her and went into our act.

"This is a representative of Walt Disney. We've received notices of your outstanding talent and want you to come to Hollywood and audition for the Mickey Mouse Club."

She fell hook, line and sinker for it. We led her on and on with increasingly fabulous offers of money, contracts and free hotel stays on Sunset Strip. We could hardly keep from laughing out loud. Finally we ran out of details and were getting annoyed that she couldn't see through it all. We broke it to her ungently. Flustered, she queried us. "Are you sure you're not from Disney?" When we identified ourselves she cried.

Somewhere along the way my father's gambling became compulsive and finances strained. Household items, bikes, radios would disappear and show up weeks or months later. When the Big Bopper and Richie Valens died in a plane crash, my best friend and I hurried home to watch *American Bandstand* and the local show *Dance Party*. In the living room, where the TV console had reigned, was an empty space. Dad had hocked the TV. At another point we placed cardboard in our shoes when they wore out too fast. I was deeply ashamed of being pitiable. I couldn't understand why my mother insisted I pray at the altar in my cardboard shoes. I tried impossibly to keep my soles flat on the floor; my cheeks burned so hard I thought they would burst. My feeling for church changed permanently though I was about to shed my neighborhood friends. My mother wisely encouraged me to make friends at church although I wondered why churches were segregated if God was above all. The girls on my block found new white friends; I became close to the three other black girls in college prep.

In a world that I had yet to understand in a larger historical context, age, family and church hemmed me in. In high school, a woman we called the white-faced lady walked about downtown. Brown-skinned, she wore white makeup smeared over her face, and hands, white clothes, stockings and shoes. It seemed like she always came right up behind us; we'd turn and gasp, even scream. We heard two explanations for her behavior: one, she was mentally unbalanced; and two, she had married a fellow white U.C. student who left her and she never got over it.

My big brother Skip, Albert H. Hart III, was named cabbie of the year in 1976 and profiled in the *SF Chronicle*. In jest, he said that, like Richard Pryor's "Bicentennial Nigger" he was the bicentennial cabbie. Skip devised a system of efficient dispatching for Yellow Cab that revolutionized the cab business and made more money for the cabbies; then he was let go. But cabbies all over the Bay area know and appreciate Skip. Every time I used to get in a cab I'd ask if the driver knew Skip. And they all did.

Although I was a four-eyed brainy girl throughout childhood—Skip busted me at a family gathering recently by saying I'd been a female Urkel—I blossomed in college. I pursued, like Urkel's character that turned into suave Steve, boyfriends, parties, a social life. I also became in my junior year a member of the Black Panther Party. I guess the "race man" impacted me subconsciously. I've translated my youthful activism during the tumultuous sixties into a lifelong passion for human rights, cultural diversity and the literary arts.

My sister grew up surrounded by mostly black families. The white families left for suburbia by the mid-60s. Once sis brought friends to hear me talk: "Doesn't she sound like the people on TV?" They agreed. Childhood was over. *Ovah.* The freedoms my parents had left Oklahoma for and fought for during WWII became backdrop for my own battles ahead: college, the assassinations, marijuana, sexual freedom, and black power. I hardly knew the tiger of death, but it too lay in wait.

THE ED SULLIVAN SHOW: The Miracle of Television

Growing up in the 50s, my siblings and I had to choose *Make Room for Daddy* or *I Love Lucy* for school night television. On Sunday nights, the whole family watched *The Ed Sullivan Show* on our one set, the high point being when a performer of our race came on. (We didn't use the word *black* in self-description then.)

The famous colored pop artists - Sammy Davis Jr., Johnny Mathis, Leslie Uggams, Dionne Warwick, and Nat King Cole - were so extraordinarily talented they seemed to glow. And yet they looked, to my adolescent eyes, like gifted pets of benevolent white mentors (Frank Sinatra, Mitch Miller, and Burt Bacharach), a status that befit the show's colorful menagerie of chimps, flamenco dancers and sensations like Elvis Presley. Colored performers and musicians who seemed of independent mind—Harry Belafonte, Richie Havens, and Odetta—had careers in folk or bluegrass further from the mainstream.

American society was one big happy family in the 1950s. A melting pot, a Jell-O & white bread land of perfection and gleaming surfaces. Not for a minute.

The truth—America was one big white out. The poet Amiri Baraka would say later the only good thing about television back then was that colored people weren't on it. There was a loss of dignity when black people entered the arena of television as maids, mammies, butlers, shoeshine boys, and had to do what white and white-minded directors and producers wanted them to do. Anyway, we weren't for the most part on TV, except for *Beulah* and a token on *Star Trek*. We were nowhere in advertising.

The 50s meant crew cuts, skinny ties, matching suits, Teen Angel, the Beachboys, the top 40 playlist, 45 rpm records, spinning the songs. But in the parallel America, Rhythm & Blues (R&B) artists were busy providing the gritty backdrop to the violence and oppression of the American dream. Rioters, marchers, protestors and regular folk followed a different drummer, doing as a popular 1964 song advised: getting "right down to the real nitty gritty." The breathlessness of the countdown to the top 15 hits on "The Lucky Strike Hit Parade" matched the breathlessness of state-sanctioned execution, which occurred with the same exciting regularity.

Amiri Baraka said the only good thing about
TV was that colored people weren't on it

1963 was a banner year for the black race. Things were heating up in the streets. That April, Martin Luther King wrote "Letter from Birmingham Jail" to white clergymen who wanted racial segregation, addressed exclusively in courts, not the streets. The next month, Bull Connor set fire hoses and attack dogs on the marchers in Birmingham. August saw The March on Washington, timed to commemorate the Emancipation Proclamation's 100th anniversary—a great peak for the Civil Rights Movement.

The miracle of television was a lucky strike for the civil rights movement. The abolitionist movement 100 years earlier had gained traction once the world, i.e. London society, understood the horror and treachery of slavery from ex-slaves like Frederick Douglass speaking abroad or from ex-slave narratives. And similarly the civil rights movement gained universal spotlight once viewers saw the hosing, brutality, flaming buses and overturned normalcy of a South under siege from arch segregationists and protestors.

The England/America exchange of influence went back and forth. At a Beatles concert in Plymouth, Great Britain, in November 1963, police used high-pressure hoses on screaming fans, a show of authority that matched the hosing of demonstrators in Birmingham six months earlier.

This hip-click to the off beat was the way black kids danced

Meanwhile, there I was, a black girl in East Oakland, playing string bass in my junior and senior high school orchestras. As we toured school festivals throughout northern California, my fellow bassist, a member of the Escovedo musical family, tried to lured me into nightclubs for $10 a night gigs. I knew better than to mention that to my strict Christian mother. But I loved music and craved it, especially Bo Diddley, Motown, and salsa. I'd dance in front of my mirror for six hours at a clip.

Diddley fused a 3-2 clave with rhythm and blues, and rock and roll. A Bo Diddley beat was clave-based, clave being the name of the patterns played on two hardwood sticks in Afro-Cuban music ensembles. This syncopated accent on the "off beat" was perfect for the click-and-slip of my pelvis as I bopped around my bedroom dance floor in my early teens. I thought I had invented a new dance until I started partying and found that this hip-click to the off beat was the way black kids danced in the Bay Area. Thank goodness for osmosis.

In 1963 Sly Stone was a hip young DJ who hadn't yet changed his birth name of Sylvester Stewart. He was fresh out of Vallejo and the CME/AME church gospel choir circuit I attended as a youth. He was firing up listeners in the San Francisco Bay Area on KSOL which he nicknamed K-SOUL. I had a painful crush on him.

My Oakland, pre 1964, was house parties, spiked punch, segregated radio and five-channel TV, servicemen getting off the ships at the Port of Oakland looking for a good time. My Oakland, post 1964, was sets (nobody said house party, they said, "Are you going to the set on Snake Rd.?"), marijuana, stoned white college boys in khakis, hippies in VW buses covered in psychedelic colors, Make Love Not War signs and longer hair on everybody. First came the swivel hipped Elvis, then Beatlemania, then the floodgates opened.

When I first heard the Beatles, I got a pure musical thrill. When I bumped into a black girl on the steps at my community college listening to "I Want to Hold Your Hand" on her plastic transistor radio, her passion, all the more strange because she was black, got my attention. Crushing on the Beatles, she held onto a .45 of the song like it was a rare gem.

Being a black urban teen, I was into Motown, the Temptations, James Brown, Chuck Berry, the Supremes and the Moonglows. I didn't crush on the Beatles like I did with Sly, Eddie Kendricks and David Ruffin. But that's the good thing about it.

Of course, I didn't know what was happening technically, that on "Please Please Please" and "I Want to Hold Your Hand," the Beatles used a double back beat, i.e. an off beat played as a one quarter note. But I knew something even better—I could dance to it. The Beatles, a convergence of R&B and pop, brought a great swinging movement from blond to dark, from privileged surfer children in the suburbs to the darkness of Liverpool's working class, an amalgam that curiously celebrated its R&B roots.

When these white females let it rip, they freed up
black women from whoredom, from bearing the
brunt and hard edge of the white man's sexuality

Neither white nor black parents could control what happened after The Pill. By the time I watched the Beatles on *Ed Sullivan* in 1964 in my parents' living room I had started college and knew a lot more about sex than I let on to my mother and father. All the prepubescent and adolescent white girls having orgasmic and orgiastic responses in public released a long suppressed sexuality from its Victorian, Southern and Puritan constraints. As these women let it rip in that prolonged moment of free public expression, they freed up black women from whoredom, from bearing the brunt and hard edge of the white man's sexuality. We were no longer the only culturally-sanctioned objects of naughty or forbidden sex, of plantation promiscuity. Stripping, nudity, free sex, skinny dipping, open marriage, group sex—sexuality came out of the closet and into the open.

Giddy with our post-high school hipness, my best friend and I regularly drove to San Francisco and hopped the cable car up to a nightclub called Copacabana West where we danced with abandon all night. I didn't know about the connection to my black roots. Or that the United States embargo against Cuba cut off Americans from overt knowledge of the Cuban influence on music, especially R&B. I just loved being able to mambo, rumba, and cha-cha with a different partner for every spin on the floor. I loved the 20 and 30 minute sets.

Before the age of 18, we had been dying to get into Finnochio's, the all-male drag nightclub in North Beach that was like forbidden fruit. Finally we got past the velvet rope. Ugh! The make-up looked caked, wigs ratty, clothing dirty and drag too uncool to be enjoyable, let alone believable. One more disassembling of the American sociocultural foundation underneath me.

Just as Finnochio's female impersonators would give way decades later to the Perpetual Sisters of Indulgence as the gay pride, sexual freedom and gender equality movements toughened up, American media and television's near complete white out would be toppled by musical, cultural and social protest.

Some look at the Beatles and say they appropriated black R&B, that they exploited it. But they acknowledged it as elemental and, by doing so, opened the door for Ike and Tina Turner, James Brown and a host of performers—once colored, now black—to share some of the rewards. Touring abroad helped many acts from the chitlin circuit beat the fabled seven year lifespan of American pop music acts and extend their showbiz longevity abroad. (Getting their health to hold out and resisting drug abuse would prove as daunting a task as overcoming segregation.)

White wasn't completely out, but black was seeping in

It only took Dick Clark until 1983 during "Motown 25: Today, Yesterday and Forever" to publically admit what was really going down in American music in the 50s and 60s: "As much as any other force in this industry, Motown caused a revolution in music. It was a quiet revolution but the ripple effect is still being felt all over the world. What Motown did was change our perception about black music and the people who made it. Now, until Motown came charging out of Detroit, about the only thing—genuinely black thing about mainstream music—was the vinyl from which the records were pressed...in the 50s and 60s, it was a common practice for white artists to take a song from a black performer and make their own version and come out with a big hit...those records were called cover records…Everybody from Elvis to an artist who later was to record for Motown, Pat Boone, did it. Until Motown, most of American record buyers didn't go looking for black records since they had hardly ever heard the real thing. By the end of 1964, most of the teenagers were dancing in the streets and they wanted Martha and the Vandellas singing to it…Kids of all colors started hitting the record stores. For Motown acts alone, they had 42 hits from which to choose. That also created a little confusion. There were certain areas that wouldn't stock an album with a black face on the cover."

With the Beatles and the British invasion, black music and rock joined for a new backdrop to the morality play called American society. White wasn't completely out, but black was seeping in. The Beatles brought black music to the foreground - on stage, front and center.

Like a slap in the smug mug of white America, the Brits acknowledged black roots. They showed how white America had unapologetically ripped off black people for centuries, never giving a whole race credit for inventing the new American art forms of jazz, gospel, blues and R&B. America never had been held accountable to blacks, morally, fiscally or legally. It's not too much to say the Beatles helped bridge the wide gulf between colored and white America.

DECIDING ON WOMANHOOD: My student activism

ALAMEDA COUNTY WELFARE DEPT.

It was spring, 1965. I had completed two years at community college and worked fulltime at the welfare department at 401 Broadway in Oakland, in the Dictaphone transcriptionist pool, while applying to SF State. Our attitude transcribing our tapes from intake workers interviewing welfare recipients was one of ridicule. They were performers, both the social workers and the clients. We laughed at their exploits. Coming from a two-parent household with a mother who was a forty-years-and-a-gold watch civil servant, I was ignorant about welfare clients holding on economically with the life preserver of Aid to Families with Dependent Children (AFDC).

DAVITA

Davita often gave me a ride home from 401; she was married to a suave, sharp dresser named Marcus. Their union came to an abrupt end when Davita insisted on keeping a second unplanned pregnancy. She carried to term in defiance of his wishes. I heard her side every day on the ride home. But, exercising his body politic, he left her. She was in control, i.e. until he left her and both kids high and dry. I saw her power evaporate in a day. It stunned her and me. How could he leave his children? Why did she insist on a second that he didn't want? I pondered their dilemma for years.

AUDREY

My cubicle partner at 401 was Audrey. The months that we worked together, two young black idealistic women, we read out loud William Goldman's *Boys and Girls Together* to the amusement of the other transcriptionists. I kept applying to SF State secret from everyone in the pool except Audrey. She had a secret too. She waited until my last day to tell me what it was. The pool threw a party for me, wishing me well as I set off for State. And finally, Audrey told me her secret--she had a son out of wedlock. She thought I would judge her because I had ridiculed the recipients. I was very ashamed that she thought I would think badly of her. Nevertheless I was eager to leave 401, where I saw civil servants looking forward to retiring in 15 or 20 years. I didn't want their future. Nor did I want to end up like Audrey or any of the clients on our Dictaphone tapes.

ALONE AND SINGING IN THE OPERA HOUSE

My first semester at San Francisco State, spring '66, was like a preliminary bout before the main fight. I rode across the Bay Bridge with fellow students from East Oakland that had attended State since high school. Their talk of parties, sororities, and fraternities, the black Greeks, didn't interest me at all. I wasn't a bourgie. I wasn't a snob. I had no wish to be a girlfriend of either. What I loved to do was catch the M streetcar into downtown after my classes, eat at Zim's at Market and Van Ness, then walk a few blocks to the War Memorial Opera House with its huge, empty, atrium. The lobby acoustics were so awe-inspiring that I'd sing my butt off for 45 minutes, my contralto like a stag horn fern in there, in transition between ancient and modern ferns. Maybe I missed my church choir rehearsals. When I switched to soprano, I was more like a maiden hair fern. Either way passersby didn't mind. In that atrium, I felt far away from judgment.

THE SPLINTERING OF THE MONOLITH

I had thought of black people as one, maybe even a monolith, though I wouldn't have used that word. I had the picture in my mind, though, of all of us being outraged, despairing, and hurt by the hosing of the children in Birmingham. Yet day after day, hearing the speakers on their soapboxes in the campus common, I was honestly bewildered by the sharp divisions in the movements. All of the revolutionary groups, the Panthers, the Nation of Islam, RAM (Revolutionary Action Movement), and the black arts poets, put down the Southern Christian Leadership Conference (SCLC), Congress of Racial Equality (CORE), National Association for the Advancement of Colored People (NAACP), and the URBAN LEAGUE as accommodationist. I heard Martin Luther King scornfully called Martin Luther Queen. The Greeks, i.e. Alphas, Kappas, Omegas, Deltas, AKAs, were dismissed as passé and bourgeois. When I went to meetings or rallies off campus, I witnessed different black guys, often in dashikis or combat fatigues, trash each other. Che Guevara with his cold-blooded executioner's rep was the model. I didn't know what to think except to be glad that, with my au naturel, nobody was attacking me. I felt like a fly on the wall trying not to get smashed. I joined the Black Students Union (BSU) that semester as it changed its name from the Negro Students Association. I really settled in my second full semester in fall of '66. A contingent of State students had gone down South to desegregate interstate buses, joining The Freedom Riders. When they returned, they radicalized the entire campus, students and faculty, practically everybody. I joined the Tutorial Program and almost instantaneously took charge of a Tutorial Center on Potrero Hill.

BERNADINE

At State, I infrequently ran into Bernadine, a pretty, light-skinned probation officer whose two kids I baby sat in high school. 32 and attending San Francisco State part time, she was a divorcee who dated a lot. My street wise father, who picked me up from her house on Sunday mornings so I could go to church, thought she was scandalous. Over her fireplace was her portrait, a Bernadine pre-beating; her ex-husband had beaten her with the spoken intent to destroy her beauty and sexual allure. She'd required hospitalization. Regardless of my father's disapproval, I admired her for retaining her allure and moxie despite the scars. She was neither a bourgie nor a militant; just a single mom earning her M.A. semester-by-semester. Her tenacity showed me that keeping one's mojo took fearlessness and disregard of other's disapproval.

MARIANNA

There was also another 32 year old at San Francisco State that I observed carefully, and this 32 year old woman was an outspoken black militant who led the BSU's name change. Her sexual liaison with a younger male student from Sacramento was the scandal of the black crowd the day he came to school with a Mohawk-long before Mohawks were popular. It was said that she had convinced him to shave his head. She was like a big, robust peony, showing off the power of sex.

GRACE

There were timid black girls there, too, like Grace, a good Catholic school girl from a family of nine children. She told everyone that she'd wanted to be a nun. She was like a delicate and brittle-stemmed sweet pea, much too vulnerable for the intense sexual politics in the BSU as well any of the Greeks. Yet, there she was, functioning as if she were a concubine of one of the brothers leading the movement, who conveniently put her up in an apartment next to his other girlfriend, with BSU monies, of course. It was all part of gaming or, rather, controlling, the system. We were all caught up in the thick of it, the sexual merry-go-round.

CECIL B. DEMILLE

Bennett, the film major from Milwaukee, hung around the commons, always there when I grabbed lunch, his half-compliments like fireflies. I had a mercurial attraction. Out of horniness, I considered giving him the key to the flesh-palace. He came from somewhere beside California and had aspiration, which placed him a step beyond instinct.

"I want to be the black Cecil B. DeMille," he said one afternoon.

"And direct a cast of thousands?" I shot back.

"That's right," he said. "Our story has never been told."

I corrected him. "Our *stories* have never been told."

He stopped as if I had placed a red light before him. "Stories...

yeah, we've got lots."

"Plenty," *Cecil*. I saw Bennett, black beret on, gentleman's cravat concealing his bony shoulder blades, directing thousands of black extras streaming around the Lincoln Memorial, the only place I'd ever seen thousands of blacks. He interrupted my dream.

"I want to shoot you," he said.

"Shoot me? Why? What did I do to you?"

"You know, take a lot of pictures," he shrugged. "Clothes on, clothes off."

"You want nudie pictures of me?"

"It's art. Art and nudity go hand in hand."

"And where would your hand go?" The mercury dropped, the door to the palace closed. Boom. Shut. He looked sheepish, not Cecil B. DeMille-ish.

CHARLOTTE

Charlotte at 16 years old began hanging around the BSU office and the Party. With her bright smile, devotion to task, Catholic school blue serge uniform and white knee socks, she proceeded to run through a host of brothers. Years later, she would become a Muslim and wear a hijab resolutely covering everything except that smile. I could sense penitence in the beautiful folds of her long robes. When I mentioned recently to one of the Central Committee that technically the brothers basically ran a train on her and were risking statutory rape, I got cussed out.

VIOLENCE AN OVERPOWERING NORM

Violence was an overpowering norm in the world with Viet Nam raging in Southeast Asia and the civil rights movement raging in the South. I began perceiving violence as a norm in the smaller world surrounding me. I tried to dodge the verbal gunfire. How could I speak scathingly of my family, church people from my childhood, even my girlfriends from high school? I tried it one time. My dad and I met up at a store, ironically called White Front in East Oakland. I repeated the rhetoric I'd heard on campus, that Negroes like him were going to end up in concentration camps because of their passivity to "the man"—the catchall term for the white man's system. Nothing could have been further from the reality of my dad's life. He had been a "race man" down South, i.e. a black man who wouldn't tolerate oppression. When he was a Tuskegee Airman in WWII, he had protested the restrictive seating in downtown Tuskegee, Al. theaters before his regiment shipped to Italy. But I was in full rebel mode, daring to sass him with the linguistic violence that had become my daily diet.

Cutting ties to our parents, the institutions of our childhood, mainly the black church, was de rigueur. One of my roomies, who called herself a black militant, returned to Third Baptist Church, San Francisco's oldest African-American church, to sing every Sunday in the choir. She was ridiculed for going but her tie remained unbroken for the rest of her life.

Nutritional violence came from the Nation of Islam. Cut your addiction to pork was the mantra. To be seen eating bacon or a ham sandwich in the school cafeteria was tantamount to being a fool. Muslims in bowties and suits surrounded the table and castigated the black students (not the whites) eating lunch. I gave up my beloved grilled ham and cheese for The Movement.

This concept of slash, give up, turn from, do away with was across the board. Physical. Emotional. Religious. Interpersonal. Linguistic violence came in the slogans and sloganeering, *Off the Pig, Black Power to Black People,* and the great ethnic change from *colored people* and *Negro* to *Black* to *African-American.* Heaven help the poor pitiful person who slipped and used the wrong term in the wrong place. But because people are only human, not everyone could live up to the strict revolutionary codes. Thus, deceits, treachery, and manipulation were part of The Movement. *Black is beautiful* was another mantra that holds to this day. My roomie asked me not to tell anyone that she used Nadinola, a skin bleaching cream I had stumbled on in her toiletries. Women who fell in love with or chose brothers who were cultural nationalists wore long dresses and elaborate African head wraps. Someone sat me down and explained that in a riot or at a protest, when the cops started swinging, I'd better be able to run fast. Ergo, jeans were feasible, not long skirts. I cut up my jeans and wore torn tee shirts, an act of wardrobe violence.

And it's not as though the women were relegated to childbearing and cooking. Kathleen Cleaver, Elaine Brown, Angela Davis, and the black women poets of the era were just as staccato and bristling as the pork-denying Muslims.

SONIA SANCHEZ

Sonia was yet another force for change. A tiny high-strung woman in her early 30s; her poetry was forceful, militant, strident, utterly sensual. My roomies and I emulated her, hung out with her, and even babysat her children until she abruptly left San Francisco amidst a romance gone sour. Sonia Sanchez commented recently on the her work in that era: "You must remember, in the time that we were writing, all the death and dying that happened and how we had discovered how much we'd been enslaved in this country…We came out hitting and slapping and alerting people to what had happened" (*The Writer's Chronicle,* Feb. 2014:29).

GWENDOLYN BROOKS

Gwendolyn Brooks, a gentler, 50 year old Pulitzer Prize winning poet, spent time on campus too, accompanying the much younger poet Don L. Lee. They carried themselves like lovers. They sat *thisclose* like lovers. It was clear she was his mentor, but to my eyes and to my roomies they were a May-December romance. She had left her long marriage soon to break with her mainstream New York publisher Harper's and embrace black cultural nationalism. Don Lee became Haki Madhubuti and his Third World Press her publisher. It was a time of dramatic change for blacks and the entire country… and me.

DECIDING ON ACTIVISM

Bobby Seale and Huey Newton came to San Francisco State

in spring, '67 to recruit at the same time Clorox, Kaiser and IBM came. The two men stood side by side, gave their spiel, their sign-up sheets laid out in the back of the room. My roommates and I, our hair au natural, in pea coats, ponchos and boots, listened. I knew the two men from community college. But I hesitated when my buddies signed to join the Black Panther Party (BPP), remembering my civil servant mother's warning about signing my name to radical causes—*never sign away your name, your body or your birthright.* While some came to call it the Summer of Love, for those of us in the belly of the beast—urban America, it was another long, hot summer. By August, I joined. On October 28, Huey and the Oakland PD got into it. One officer died; Huey was shot and charged with charged with murder and assault. The BPP goes into its next evolution, Free Huey, the campaign that Eldridge creates. It's as bloody and violent as childbirth, and I'm in the middle of it.

We five young women were the first wave of students from San Francisco State to join the Black Panther Party. We were referred to as sisters with skills. Evelyn handled finances, Janice became Bobby Seale's scheduler, Betty managed the BPP office, and Jo Ann corralled the troops. I worked on the BPP Intercommunal Newspaper with Eldridge. We remain enrolled but spend our waking hours with the BPP in the office, in the community. Our nine-room flat on Potomac St overlooking Duboce Park, unbeknownst to us Alcoholics Anonymous first meeting place, would turn into a BPP safe house. But first, I start reading the BPP paper. It was interesting, nothing like, not even remotely, the Oakland Tribune or the San Francisco Chronicle. Nothing like what I had learned in journalism classes. It wasn't objective. In the back of my mind, I had wondered what objective meant when the front page, the inside, the obituaries, the society columns, the advertisements all reflected the World According to the White Man. Only on the sports pages black faces and names appeared. The more I read the BPP paper the more it fascinated me.

KATHLEEN CLEAVER

We meet up, the roomies and I, on the landing of the admin building at State. We just got married, Eldridge tells us, pride of ownership all over his face. She comes off shy like a bride but coiled like a panther; she is high yellow, green-eyed, with a puffed brown sugar natural, black boots and turtleneck, wired for takeoff. The green eyes speak to us. They say: get back. She extends a smile. I hear him say: she was George Ware's secretary. I can't see her taking care of nobody's stuff. That's what we're here for.

AGENT PROVOCATEURS???

These two guys from SNCC in LA—or who said they were from SNCC in LA, visited the BSU offices at State, ultra-cool, ultra-blasé revolutionaries wearing the hell out of their regulation overalls and denim jackets I had been busy getting my paycheck, didn't have time to listen to their rap. I was trying to get paid not laid. When I got back from the bank, they were still holding court. The large one was vociferous, the quiet one smiled at what was being said. I thought they were talking about organizing the South, maybe the ultimate cattle prod story, judging from how captivated people looked. But the big guy was going on about sex as calmly as if he was recommending vaccination. "Mothers should give their young sons head and fathers should initiate young daughters into the mysteries of oral copulation." I couldn't believe my ears.

People looked disgusted and walked out. I don't know why I stayed, I didn't agree with him. "Parents have to show their children the way of the world. A parent can do it gently, wisely, slowly." He used his hands graphically. More people walked. "this is too important to leave to chance or strangers" It made sense, but it didn't make sense.

The two of them looked, talked, walked, and moved like movement people but maybe they weren't. Maybe they were agents. Maybe they were evil. Once I joined the BPP, they taught us that agents and agent-provocateurs always proposed the most extreme, most outlandish action, and more derring-do than deliberate. At the moment it intrigued me.

THE FIRST MARTYR LIL BOBBY

I cry picturing Lil Bobby, scared in the basement, refusing to take off his clothes to save his ass, prison-savvy Eldridge stripping naked, emerging into the lethal spotlight. The peacock lived, the peachick died. The brothers in P.E. class who were there talk of a volley of bullets electrifying Lil Bobby. Lynching up north. The panthers wore indigo and black; the cops wore indigo and black, a brotherhood of measure.

LUMPEN PROLETARIAT SHIT

I shoplift a boatload of shit, books, records, clothes, scarves, grades. I get quite good at it, a master, the good girl-turned-slippery eel until I got caught. My shoplifting case gets postponed for several months, at my repeated requests, hoping the BPP would come to my rescue magically. They're fighting big battles, political battles, life and death battles. But Bobby Seale sits me down, listens to my story and tells me about a 50-foot area outside the store. If I was arrested inside the area, which I was, I can plead not guilty on the grounds that I had forgotten to pay. Bobby instructs me on how to question the store manager and emphasize that he never asked if I had stolen something and didn't discuss it while we waited for the police. I feel a bit ashamed to take up his time, but Bobby handles it like it was routine.

Am I a common thief, I ask myself, when I see the lumpen proletariat in court, stammering, confessing, begging for mercy. A young man who stole a deck of cards, worth less than a dollar--30 days in Santa Rita County Jail; a young white woman who confessed to stealing a $5 bathing suit from Woolworth's--six months on the prison farm; a black man who burglarised, a white girl who left the scene of an accident, a Latino youth who stole petty cash from an employer--jail, jail, jail. I am petrified; everybody is getting time. The courtroom clears out, leaving the prosecutor, store manager, judge, court reporter, all white, and me. Using Bobby's strategy and my best collegiate voice I take the stand. The judge allows me to ask questions of the manager who can't remember what he asked me outside the store. He didn't know how many feet I had gone before being stopped. I get the feeling that he had expected a repeat of the past two hours--stammering hasty inarticulate confessions.

My thoughts flow in two streams. In my pounding heart, I want to confess everything. But I don't want to end up under the jail. Instead I talk school, grades, reading, wanting to teach, making an honest mistake, forgetting what I'd picked up in the store until after I'd been stopped outside. The judge smiles as if lulled by either the late afternoon or my Future Teachers of America voice. He reduces the charge to malicious mischief, a misdemeanour, and fines me $25. I walk out, relieved to be free

DECIDING ON ABORTION

By 1968, I am a senior at San Francisco State when I have to see about my period. I see the people at Planned Parenthood. I am so busy on deadline for the Black Panther Party intercommunal newspaper and working part-time at UCSF Medical Center that I forget to go back for the results. Between visits I tell my roomie. I know she has a sympathetic mind. And that's what I need, not someone to tell me what to do.

I ask her to go horseback riding with me on Skyline Blvd. in Oakland. Horseback riding was one of the classy dates, classy that is at the start of an affair. But if you got pregnant, so I heard, horseback riding dislodged the fetus, made you abort. We go early the next day. I ride my horse at a gallop, enough to bounce up and down, enough to bring a period down. It hurts but I have to do it. She rides her horse like a mule, poking along. No blood. Planned Parenthood (PP) closes on the weekend.

I can't wait for a yes or a no. She watches as I take Carter's little liver pills by the tens. Maybe I can get sick and have my stomach pumped. I have never been sick. I don't know anything but good health. I take 100 Carter's little liver pills. I feel a slight nausea, nothing more than I've felt on and off for weeks. I don't go to the hospital. I don't get pumped. I show up at PP bright and early. They give it to me, the dim late words: you're expecting. No, don't tell me

I'm pregnant. I only screwed once in this whole time period. The dr. says: "It's the Immaculate Conception, we hear about it all the time."

The next two weeks are frantic. I know I'm pregnant, no one else knows. If I don't tell anyone, then no one else ever has to know. I gather options:

- leave the country and have an abortion in Norway (this from a doctor to a student);
- keep doing bodily damage until I either abort or kill myself;
- drink quinine;
- get the coat hanger.

I'm afraid. I can't hurt myself anymore. A woman at the PP said I could have crippled myself with the liver pills. She gives me a number to call. I'm afraid. Maybe she's the FBI, trying to get me to commit suicide. Maybe she's not the FBI but has contacts with abortionists, dirty-fingered men in bare-light-bulb offices. I'm afraid. I'm out of money. I go back up to UCSF Med Center to get my severance check.

When Jennifer, the 9th floor switchboard operator, greets me like old times, she thanks me for giving her my dress. (I didn't give her anything, I left it there. The RNs must have given it to her). But she is happy to see me, says, you were so different, it's so dull now. She looks at me closely, says, you look worried, what's wrong? I start to tell her and hear my voice waver; she's the first person in the City besides my roomies to show concern for me. She pulls out a memo.

It explains a new law in California permitting abortion to be legal and performed by doctors in hospitals. She gives me a number to call. It's an abortion shrink. She says I have to visit him twice, talk with him. I frown. She says, it's more a formality...but when you go, especially the second visit, talk like it's already driving you nuts, being pregnant...act a little crazy or paranoid or something like that... then he can sign and you can get it done at Kaiser.

I end up, nearly three months along, sitting in his office in Berkeley, talking as nutty and paranoid as I can. I tell him about the sirens in San Francisco; about the FBI outside my apartment; about the teacher from high school and his photos of the dead swallowed man and the train-cut in-half man and how only recently they have turned back up in my dreams; I tell him about all the agent provocateurs in the Party who make my skin crawl; I tell him about my fears. I don't have to exaggerate.

I ask him, is this enough? He nods and signs the second trimester abortion form and walks me out of the reception area. I see through the reflection in the windows the shrink standing, gaping. I don't know if it's what I told him or that he's seeing an actual live Panther.

In June 1967, the California Legislature passes the Therapeutic Abortion Act, California becoming the third state in the country after North Carolina and Colorado to legalize abortions. An estimated 18,000 illegal abortions occur annually in California, and illegal abortions are a major factor in maternal deaths. While women with money, i.e. middle-class, can get foreign or safe non-hospital abortions, poor women perform self-induced abortions or leave the task to unlicensed helpers. Nearly 80 percent of all abortion deaths occur among non-Caucasian women.

I am in the middle of my second trimester when Kaiser admits me. The California Abortion Act has a 20 week limitation from the time of conception after which a therapeutic abortion may not be given for any reason. My parents, alerted by my use of their health coverage, come to see me, disapproving but loving.

Finally, I head away from death. My abortion, the violent disposal of an unwanted baby, will change my feelings forever about sex and sexuality. But, for the now, I barely take a day off from my pressing revolutionary duties at the newspaper. Such is the life of a twenty-one year- old black activist/movement worker in Oakland in 1968. Echoing in my ear is the refrain I put in a headline for the BPP newspaper from H. Rap Brown, "Violence is as American as cherry pie."

Emory, the BPP's artist and I put the paper together; he shows me how to hand-letter headlines, pressing out Instatype; cut and paste. We work at ease; kind and talented, his absolute devotion to the party guides what we do; we do it all, it seems. Emory and Matilaba do all the artwork, I type anything handwritten that needs to go to the typesetters and assist with the layout. Huey, Bobby, Eldridge give us items; speeches, addresses, position papers. Huey and Eldridge write prolifically from jail. We use solicited articles, telegrams from the famous and notable, poetry, rally news, announcements, quotes from the pantheon at will—Mao, Fanon, Marx, Che. I proudly layout a Western Union telegram from Betty Shabazz.

BETTY SHABAZZ

718APST APR 12 68 LD081L 0LB088 DL PDB TOOL MTVERNON NY 12 711A PST.

BOBBY JAMES HUTTON FAMILY, CARE KATHLEEN CLEAVERS   850 OAK St OAKLAND CALIF THE QUESTION IS NOT WILL IT BE NON-VIOLENCE VERSUS VIOLENCE BUT WHETHER A HUMAN BEING CAN PRACTICE HIS GOD GIVEN RIGHT OF SELF-DEFENSE.SHOT DOWN LIKE A COMMON ANIMAL HE DIED A WARRIOR FOR BLACK LIBERATION. IF THE GENERATION BEFORE HIM HAD NOT BEEN AFRAID HE PERHAPS WOULD BE ALIVE TODAY. REMEMBER LIKE SOLOMON THERE IS A TIME FOR EVERYTHING. A TIME TO BE BORN, A TIME TO DIE, A TIME TO LOVE, A TIME TO HATE, A TIME TO FIGHT AND A TIME TO RETREAT. IN THE NAME OF BROTHERHOOD AND SURVIVAL REMEMBER BOBBY. IT COULD BE you YOUR SON YOUR HUSBAND OR YOUR BROTHER TOMORROW. CRIMES AGAINST AN INDIVIDUAL ARE OFTEN CRIMES AGAINST AN ENTIRE NATION. TO HIS FAMILY ONLY TIME CAN ELIMINATE THE PAIN OF LOSING HIM BUT MAY HE BE REMEMBERED IN THE HEARTS AND MINDS OF ALL US. BETTY SHABAZZ

I feel comforted. She is mother to all that swirls around her fallen husband's words. We take amphetamines near deadline so we can make it. When I shit, I cannot believe the foot and a half-length of my stools. I go three days without sleep, my skin itching in spite of showers.

KATHLEEN

The roomies and I go to Eldridge's one morning, waiting for Kathleen. When she comes in the room, she has the same look she wore when we were first introduced. We see her beauty marks, the black and blue ones; this morning they're on her legs. We get the elbows to going, the eyes to rolling. Sometimes they're on her arms. Sometimes her face. I wish somebody would try to beat on me like a damn drum; I don't care how famous his ass is. This is repellent… and entertaining. We talk about it casually; everyone does.

In jail, behind the glass, Eldridge says he wishes Kathleen had an automatic beating machine so she could beat herself while he's gone.

ED AND VIOLENCE

I didn't know break-and-entry as in the BSU brothers breaking into the school paper at State throwing punches at the white boys could lead to night fright (when a guy can't get it up, you know), didn't know about that until the entire central committee of the BSU, including my boyfriend, got it, performance anxiety, erectile dysfunction. They didn't know they had it either. Each one thought only he had it with one of us who was his lady or, I suppose, the second lady or for heaven's sake, the third. I thought it was my fault. He thought it was my fault. We thought it was my fault. I tried to open wider, suck smoother, talk softer until the grapevine started dropping rumoricious little grapes. One by one it turned out none of the brothers could get it up. It wasn't me. It wasn't us. It was the inexplicable working of fright. Scare the hell out of somebody else. You scare the hell out of yourself.

THE CASTE SYSTEM AS INTERPERSONAL VIOLENCE

The natural hairdo formed a caste system, with "straight-haired sisters" being relegated and called out even. A poem my roomie had written and had me read often got round applause and hoots. It had a popular line belittling sisters with Vidal Sassoon haircuts and go-go boots.

Skin color was a holdover caste from centuries of mulatto privilege...The top women in the BPP, the ones with visibility and prominence, were Kathleen Cleaver, Ericka Huggins, Elaine Brown, and Angela Davis, all light skinned.

Of the BSU brothers on the Central Committee, most had light skinned girlfriends and wives or partners lighter-skinned than themselves. In my case, my brownness contrasted with my boyfriend-then-husband who was dark-skinned.

• Alma was the wife of the second president of the Black Student Union. She was a personal friend, our commonality being our men on the BSU Central Committee. We had our first babies at the same time. She was a dynamite cook and we often cooked meals together. She and Bennie had married before he started his activist phase. She had striking shoulder-length, pressed and permed hair and wore it defiantly. The brothers were relentless in pushing her to go au natural. She adamantly refused. I proudly wore my natural but had a laissez-faire attitude about other women's hairdos. Live and let live, I thought; the advent and popularity of the natural hairdo meant that, finally, black women were freed up from the hot comb and could choose to fashion their hair as they chose. I still feel that way. One of the biggest arguments in my relationship came when my man, who loved Alma's cooking, disparaged her one evening while we were at home talking. I pointed out the hypocrisy of sitting at her table, eating her food, yet disrespecting her personhood. He scoffed at my reasoning. We went back and forth. I picked up a large glass ashtray (neither of us smoked cigarettes but lit up weed on the regular). I heaved it at him. Luckily he ducked because it hit the door and left a dent in the wood. Astounded, he said, "You're the kind of woman my father warned me about. He said a woman who can't use her fists is far more dangerous because she'll pick up something that can kill you." I was as astounded as he was at my gut violence; that I was as capable of violence as anyone else.

• Several semesters after the Black Studies Dept. had been established, most of the Central Committee brothers graduated and transitioned from being the most powerful people on an 18,000 student campus, leaders of the longest student strike in the history of American higher education, and developers of the nation's first Black Studies Department. They became regular college graduates looking for work. Several came up with a scheme for counterfeit money. My guy brought some of the bills with our household money. I thought it looked patently bogus and told him to take it around the corner to the Chinese grocer. He did, and the person behind the counter passed it back to him without saying a word. However, the FBI and the CIA were watching all of us. We were revolutionaries. The FBI got wind of the counterfeit scheme and called in the brothers one by one for interrogation. Of the bunch, only D. broke down and gave up names. One brother ended up doing time for a year. The rest of them, the Central Committee, cold-shouldered D. for snitching. Alma and I thought they were being harsh and used pillow talk for nearly a year to get them to relent. Finally they did, and D. was embraced again.

SEXUAL POLITICS OR SEXUAL BOUTIQUE?

The role of women and sexuality within revolutionary movements of the 1960s and 1970s impacted me as both participant and witness. I was a student activist and political activist in several movements, including the country's ground-breaking Black Student Union at SFSU from 1966-1972, the Black Panther Party from 1967-1969, and the nation's first Black Studies Department at SFSU from 1969-1970. Our sexual presence, acquiescence, devotion, willingness, and escapades supported each of these revolutions. Women used their sexuality and sexual relationships to support and sustain the revolutionary activities. At San Francisco State during the revolution of the 60s, BSU brothers ran guns and women. One who set his harem up in adjacent apartments, and graced one of my roomies with his majestic virility, had the nerve to tell me, decades later after I wrote *Virgin Soul*, that my account of sexual escapades wasn't valuable to the history of the revolution of the sixties because they were secondary to the revolution. Bullshit! Our sexual devotion, escapades and all, made revolution bearable. When I told another brother from the revolution about

- A pair of young sisters from Seattle attending Mills College, high yellow and high bourgie, lived in a swank apartment facing Lake Merritt. Brothers couldn't resist. They too were run through sexually.

- A teenage volunteer, no more than 14, high yellow and voluptuous, was snatched by Eldridge who ravished her for three days. When her mother came to the BPP office looking for her, my roomies made excuses for her disappearance and simultaneously pressured the brothers to make Eldridge return her to the office, which he did.

He was incredulous. That's why I write about it here. Future activists need to see the fuller picture. Sexual dynamics make the world go around and they make revolutions occur. Women's sexuality, childbirths and abortions, and sexual politics were integral parts of these movements. However, there were also tensions and debates around the value and role of women's sexual exploits within the movements.

In 1967, I threw my birth control pills down the toilet, in an act of rebellion against being a pawn for black male sexuality. I would wait for love with a man who wanted me exclusively. It took a while to find that kind of love.

At Bread Loaf Writers Conference in 2012, I read a chapter of *Virgin Soul*, my semi-autobiographical novel documenting the black revolution that established Black Studies as a discipline. Several white women came up to me at Bread Loaf and said they went through the exact same thing in SDS (Students for a Democratic Society) and YSA (Young Socialists Alliance). I read Che Guevara's biography, *Che Guevara: A Revolutionary life* and saw the exact same phenomenon. Why is it so hard to face that using young women and their sexual vulnerability, their adoration of the top dogs and the simultaneous oppression of them, is key to everything political?

Much time would pass before I was able to write about it,

and even then fiction was the means to voice that trauma, as if my unbridled voice and witness was too much. I created a character, an alter ego, Mimi, in one story that revisited the sixties scene in retrospect:

> Mimi had felt uncomfortable the last time she had visited the Big House, as the Black Student Union had named a two-story Victorian in the Fillmore district in San Francisco. Guys were doing lines, rolling joints, watching a porno movie playing on the wall, the same brothers who had led the longest student strike in history at State and established the nation's first black studies program there, the very same brothers who had faced off the police in Hunter's Point, West Oakland and East Palo Alto, the same brothers who finagled student body funds and bought guns for the Black Panther Party, who just a decade previous had been all over sisters with naturals and averse to sisters with pressed hair. A vision of a woman's creamy white butt and pink nipples crammed the wall in the darkened room. Someone had turned off the soundtrack, so the woman's moaning and coming hard as rocks could be imagined from her mouth opening wide and her body convulsing. Miles' quintet blasted "Nefertiti" from the stereo. That was the way Mimi had learned to get high: Turn off the TV and its white noise. Keep the set on. Put Miles or Coltrane on the box and start rolling. The politics, demonstrations, rage, cries for society to explode with justice for all, had come down to this. Sex on the wall. White sex.
>
> "Why are brothers who're supposed to be so damn hip to the ways of the white man—and so Black—playing divine music to Miss Ann's naked behind?" Mimi had protested. But no one was taken with what she had to say as if she had become soundless as the epoch had faded.

A move to the East Coast and a fractious divorce led me to become Buddhist. Thereupon, I began to examine my predilection for turmoil, violent upheavals, and severing ties with people. It was sobering. Other people, society, my parents, and lovers ceased being my culprits. It took deep self-reflection to face the culprit within.

FIVE COMRADES IN THE BLACK PANTHER PARTY, 1967-1970

Bobby Seale and Huey Newton came to San Francisco State in the spring of '67 to recruit at the same time Clorox, Kaiser and IBM came. The two men stood side by side, gave their spiel, their sign-up sheets laid out in the back of the room. My roommates and I wore our hair natural and favored pea coats, hip ponchos and boots. But I hesitated when they signed to join the BPP, remembering my civil servant mother's warning about signing my name to radical causes.

While some came to call it the Summer of Love, for those of us in the belly of the beast—urban America, it was another long, hot summer. In August I joined.

We five young women became the first wave of students from San Francisco State to join the Black Panther Party. We were referred to as sisters with skills. Evelyn handled finances, Janice became Bobby Seale's scheduler, Betty managed the BPP office, and Jo Ann corralled the troops. I worked on the BPP Intercommunal Newspaper with Eldridge and Kathleen Cleaver.

Some of the first issues of the paper were laid out at The Black House. It's no coincidence that that stately Victorian on Broderick St. was a prime gathering spot for poetry readings, jazz sets and political talks; poets, dancers, musicians, students, party people and the lumpen mixed and mingled for a time at this home of Eldridge Cleaver and poet-playwright Marvin X. The Black House unity didn't last; the cultural nationalists, who advocated a black-only cultural milieu, and the militant Panthers, who welcomed alliances with radical whites, split.

The Panthers were creating a new language, what Jean-Paul

Sartre calls superlanguage. Sartre calls it language distortion, a means by which the colonized deconstruct their oppression and reorder existence. Police became *pigs*; a deadly police raid became *a reign of terror*. We made the language, as Sartre identifies it, revolutionary and incantatory: *Off the pigs. Power to the people. All power to the people. Free Huey.*

Our gang of five affected policy and high-level decisions by virtue of our intense participation, outspokenness, our spacious Potomac St. flat which became a safe house, our connections to our families and communities in Oakland, Hunters' Point, the Sunset and Fillmore districts, and Iowa [shout out to Janice] where we grew up. Our parents and relatives provided money, housing, books, cars, meeting places, food and clothing to the party as documented by the FBI.

We also formed liaisons and romantic relationships with brothers in the party. From the upper echelon to the lumpen proletariat, we lived, slept, ate and cooked with the BPP, running up and down the state and the country, all of which was a natural development that resulted in many discussions on Potomac St. about the differences [and similarities] between brothers from the street and brothers on campus. We were the initial link between the campus and the party. Three of us married "brothers in the struggle" who also happened to be educated brothers. This is significant because our connections and intimacy [which some labeled promiscuity] connected brothers from the party with brothers from SF State. The BSU brothers like to talk about supplying the BPP with guns and money, but *this bridge called my back* supplied the people's army with equal and greater provision.

When Huey was arrested and jailed in the shootout in November 1967, the paper overnight became an international organ, and the BPP an international sensation. To the world the party surfaced as the radical arm of the civil rights movement. At that point, my work stepped up with the paper. Donations poured into the office for the Free Huey movement. Police and FBI surveillance intensified. Six months later, the killing of Bobby Hutton and the shooting/jailing of Eldridge led to a meeting outside in Mosswood Park in Oakland, across the street from Kaiser Permanente Hospital. We met in the park because we didn't want the FBI to hear the tape from Huey. On it, he reorganized the party, and to my surprise, appointed me editor-in-chief during Eldridge's jail stay.

This changed all the dynamics. School became irrelevant. SF State had been indifferent and even hostile to Negro students for so long that the strongest sense of belonging had come from black sororities and fraternities. However, after going down South and participating in the Freedom Rides in the summer of 1966, a multiracial contingent of students returned to radicalize the campus. Those students developed the Tutorial Program at SF State into a community-based web of free after school tutoring centers in the Mission, Fillmore and Potrero Hill. This campus program was a first concrete radicalization for many. My roommates and I tutored and ran several of the centers.

Many idealistic students in the sixties dropped out and some devoted lives to the movement; by the time they returned to campus, many had changed their class affiliation. My friends and I dropped out and worked in the BPP full time. We eventually returned to campus too, armed, not only with actual weapons, but with a new consciousness about education, service, the poor, the police and the military, oppression, and civil and human rights. Our experience in the party helped us envision a viability in revitalizing and connecting to our community versus fleeing into the mainstream, corporate America or the professions as a distanced, glancing downward teacher or social worker. No matter our background, and all five of us came from two-parent, middle-class families, we became aware of the class contradictions in the American dream.

I saw Bobby Seale recently and had to remind him who I was by recalling the roommates. He said, quite sincerely, "Which one was my girlfriend?" I wasn't insulted. After all, he was looking back 40 years, and we were far more than girlfriends.

IN THE BEGINNING

I had just had my baby boy in August, 69, and begun teaching at the college level that same month, so my mother-in-law kept my baby while I went to the Breakfast for Children Program   And I did hear, *why are you taking care of other people's children instead of your own baby?* even though they adored the new baby and I was breastfeeding. But that was the zeitgeist, the cultural climate of the era. The Free Breakfast for Children Program, the core of the party's Survival Programs, was a community service program run by the Black Panther Party. It provided a free breakfast before school. The Party announced it would begin in September 68 and launched it in January 1969 at St. Augustine's Episcopal Church in Oakland, Father Earl Neill's church. A church member Ruth Beckford-Smith, the Bay Area's premiere interpreter of modern African dance, was in charge of this first program.

It had sprung from the vision of Party founders Huey P. Newton and Bobby Seale, inspired by the essential role of breakfast for learning and the belief that alleviating hunger and poverty was necessary for Black liberation. The program was a direct response to the war on poverty in the 60s, the U.S. government's promise to provide basic needs (housing, food, safety) to its citizens.

Ruth Beckford and Father Neil constructed a healthy menu and a kitchen and dining hall that passed health inspections. The program's launch day served 11 children. By the end of the week 135 children were being served daily. Volunteers would start setting up and around 6 am and served the meal from 7-8:30. A typical breakfast included bacon, eggs, grits, pancakes, toast, sausage, juice or milk. Pretty soon the Program was mandatory in all chapters nationwide. In one year, the Panthers were feeding over 10,000 children every day.

And then there was success.

At community centers and churches, the breakfasts inspired children and parents to learn about black liberation and the Black Panther Party. We provided transportation to some sites for children, from home to the site, then to school. The party used the program to educate children and families about anti-capitalism, Black pride, and developing revolutionary consciousness. Many programs in predominantly Black neighborhoods served children of all ethnicities. We volunteers from the party worked alongside community members, brothers feeding children too. From 1966-1982, two-thirds of party members were women. We highlighted the inadequacies of the federal government to support even public school lunch programs.

I've had adults come up to me at speaking engagements and thank me for helping feed them as children.

So there we were fixing grits and eggs, donated by local businesses, [some of whom, yes, we did have to strong-arm]. The War in Vietnam was raging. The anti-war movement was raging equally,

Then came the destruction.

FBI DIR. J. Edgar Hoover targeted the Black Panther Party as the greatest threat to domestic security, calling us domestic terrorists. He wanted to destroy the Breakfast Program because it was effective and popular. He said, in 1969:

> One of our primary aims in counterintelligence as it concerns the [Black Panther Party] is to keep this group isolated from the moderate black and white community which may support it….This is most emphatically pointed out in their Breakfast for Children Program, where they are actively soliciting and receiving support from uninformed whites and moderate blacks.

So, federal authorities worked to discredit the Breakfast

Program. They worked to destroy the Party through COINTELPRO. They targeted the party with rumors of poisoned food. They raided breakfast program locations while children were eating. The FBI widely denounced it as "as a front for indoctrinating children with Panther propaganda".[Hoover wrote: "The [Breakfast Program] represents the best and most influential activity going for the BPP and, as such, is potentially the greatest threat to efforts by authorities to neutralize the BPP"

Thus the US government gave police nationwide, the FBI, and federal agents, permission and encouragement to harass and discredit the program, the people it benefited, and the Party itself. This is all well-documented, similar to records kept by the Nazis during the Holocaust.

One FBI raid in Chicago ended with smashing and urinating on all the food that was to be used for the breakfast program.

FBI and local police raids, arrests, and murders of Panther leaders as well as party infighting led to the closure of most Panther chapters and the end of the Free Breakfast Program in the 1970s. Seattle's program closed in 1977.

But the US government and legislators understood that it helped reduce hunger and food insecurity and implemented a national breakfast program built on the framework of the Panthers' and efforts led by the women's movement.

The Free Breakfast for Children Program was one of 60+ community social programs of the Black Panther Party, renamed Survival Programs in 1971, operated by party members under the slogan "survival pending revolution".

A BADGE OF HONOR: Being a Panther, being anonymous

I joined the Black Panther Party at 20. My unique life path became public 45 years later, in 2013 when my semi-autobiographical novel about a radical student in the Bay Area who joins the Party, *Virgin Soul*, was published. My anonymity ended. I was never ashamed of being a Panther. To the contrary, it's been a badge of honor that I fought against police oppression and brutality. I believe we helped avert large-scale urban warfare in my hometown, Oakland. Moving from California to New Jersey in 1972, I never hid my Panther past. My dearest friends in New Jersey and New York City knew my life. One called me Little Miss Anonymity; another who believed in my writing called me Miss Big Bubba Tubba. Another at a dinner party, much to my chagrin, introduced me as The Panther Queen. I didn't think that colorful chapter in my youth defined me, yet, after a while, I realized I was hiding in plain sight. I had chosen to be an observer not an exclaimer. Why? It had to do with fear, hostility and confrontation. The party confronted the most powerful and the deadliest force in the civilized world, the U.S. government, and got decimated by COINTELPRO, J. Edgar Hoover's vicious suppression of the BPP. I was busy being a wife, mother and then divorced single parent.

In dozens of interviews for *Virgin Soul*, I was asked about this essential part of me that theretofore had been known by family and close friends. I had been embedded deeply in the Party's infrastructure, editing the weekly newspaper, helping serve at the Breakfast for Children, visiting inmates in San Quentin prison. In the student movement at San Francisco State, I had edited the strike journal at State during the historic 4-1/2 month student strike that revolutionized higher education and brought black and ethnic studies into being. I graduated college, married, had a child, and taught in the black studies department for a year. It was a glorious period in my life, a time to be free, open, above ground with everything - politics, sex, love, my body. Then it was over. Like many other radicals who were rank and file, I had to get on with the business of life, work, find places to live, make new friends. Why did I not bravely and honestly proclaim my participation in the Party? Although the Panthers have become accepted as a force for positive change, this took fifty years. Many of us lived in anonymity [and under FBI scrutiny] throughout the intervening decades. Those who were "out" suffered social exclusion, jail time, exile, ostracism, and poverty.

I moved back east at 26 years of age in what a chum called The Big Spread. We had been powerful students during the campus unrest, but once we graduated we couldn't even get entry-level jobs because of our politics. Many of us moved away, some abroad, radical whites to Mendocino and Ukiah. For me, life took twists and turns, no one was interested in my radical past. I suffered a near fatal fall and ended up in New York's Columbia Presbyterian Hospital for two weeks and a subsequent eight months of physical therapy to regain mobility. The orthopedic surgeon prepping to operate told me that I was getting the exact operating team (for free) that had just performed surgery on Mayor John Lindsay who had fallen off his bike in Central Park. In the hospital I met a jazz singer, renowned in Europe, who had surgery on her leg that was stitched up Frankenstein-like, groin to ankle. She sang for us. Beautifully. Another woman whose husband beat her hand with a baseball bat held it up for all to see; it looked like a catcher's mitt. On the ward, I saw human suffering up close, closer than ever before.

Revealing my true identity was a balancing act of candor v. consequences, all the more so moving from the liberal Bay Area to New Jersey.

Even in a job at a progressive non-profit, I didn't reveal who I was until I became good friends with the executive director's administrative assistant. She and I became lifelong friends. Likewise, with my social life, I made friends cautiously. I was mortified when that one friend introduced me at a dinner party as "the Panther Queen"; this same person, who also had participated in sixties radicalism, dubbed me "little miss anonymity." Whether intentional or not, she forced me to evaluate the worth of my experiences.

The cast of characters, the set of experiences, I encountered in New Jersey overshadowed the events of my early twenties.

- My friend, the executive's admin asst., approached me, knowing how hard I was struggling as a single parent. She knew an immigrant trying to get status who would pay me $7,500 to marry so he could become legal. I refused, not thinking about it twice. When another acquaintance did get into this kind of set up, the man paid her $7,000. But he and his friends/countrymen beat her up and disfigured her so badly she had to have plastic surgery.

- I met a woman and her tribe of foster and natural children. They all used, not napkins, but the same towel to wipe their hands at dinner. At first repulsed, I came to see true love and caring in their household.

- I met Marcela from Peru, a go-go dancer whose white, insanely jealous boyfriend beat her regularly. She told me it was hard for a stripper to keep a boyfriend. She and I bonded. Marcela's father was an upper middle-class dentist in Peru who couldn't speak English well and would never be able to take the U.S. boards. One Thanksgiving Marcela invited me to her home but asked me to come in the side entrance because her mother was prejudiced against dark people, not just blacks, even dark skinned Hispanics. This infuriated me. But friendship was precious. I kept quiet to Marcela's face. Being two-faced suited many parts of my life.

- For a time, I lived in a Rahway high rise, the Rahway State Prison visible from my balcony. Next door, I made friends with a woman in the Nation of Islam whose children were my son's playmates. I met other Muslims who frequented the mosque in E. Orange while running schemes on Rt. 22, floating bad checks and stolen credit cards to buy bookcases to hold the Holy Koran. I recalled how, in the Party, Eldridge Cleaver, an ex-convict himself, had called those who robbed and stole "lumpen proletariat." In BPP political education classes, we learned that Karl Marx said that people from the lowest stratum of the industrial working class would join the revolution and bring their ways with them. It would be our task to reeducate them.

• I went with my neighbor to visit a young Black Muslim woman who had just had surgery. Some sisters, covered head to toe, made more over their headdresses and matching dresses than helping the woman who could barely walk. When they went in the kitchen, they brought her something to drink. I took the drink back to the kitchen which was purely filthy. I exploded at the women: "Where is your religion that you can't help her clean this house? What is the purpose of your allegiance to clothes and not to people in need?" I did what I could but had to go clean my own house. The ideals of my twenties were eclipsed by real life.

• A friend never revealed he was gay but a mutual friend saw him at *The Color Purple* film premiere standing in line French-kissing another man. I was perplexed. We laughed and talked about seemingly everything. He knew all about me. Why couldn't he come out to me? It took years before I recognized the parallel between his closet and my closet.

• This same friend asked several of us to hold a small dinner for his sister from Tennessee. I welcomed her into my home; we made nice over a delicious meal. The more we talked, the more evident it became that she was rightwing. While my friends and I eyeballed each other, she proclaimed her anti-abortion stance and support of the murder of abortion doctors. I never expected a black, sweet-faced relative of a close friend would be a raving fanatic. I got a taste of how I looked to my own family when I had joined the Party.

- My husband, child, and I visited the Nation of Islam's Muhammad Mosque no.7 in Harlem. This Cali girl was in heaven on 125th St. I was so not a believer, but I understood what the Nation was doing: Do for Self. Yessss. I was savvy enough to wear long dresses and cover my head. Another woman, not so savvy, came in a short dress, her hair uncovered. Minister Louis Farrakhan singled her out, verbally chastising her in front of the several hundred present. I felt her humiliation. It reminded me of the divide in the sixties between black cultural nationalists and the Black Panther Party. Each had a code and woe to those who violated it.

I never hid my Panther past. I even wrote short stories about the tumultuous sixties. But converting from journalism and teaching to fiction was difficult. I determined in 1980 to join a writing workshop. 34 years young, I grabbed a sheaf of poems to take to my first writing workshop since college. I was so ecstatic that I forgot I was black until I saw a living room full of white people. They warmly greeted me, kicking off a 25 year process of developing my craft. The more I wrote, the more confidence I gained. I showed people stories, but never a whole manuscript.

One day in 1984, I was subbing in a social studies classroom in my son's jr. high school in Ridgewood, New Jersey. I opened the teacher's lesson plans. He had collected newspaper and magazine articles into a plastic folder that I thumbed through, astonished. I saw my life in-a whole unit of study on the Black Panther Party in suburbia! Questions he had formulated for his students showed he was left-leaning and earnest. I felt comfortable to share my BPP experiences with the students who were as astonished as I was. I'd had no contact with the BPP since moving to New Jersey in 1972, yet here it was. My past. I realized *I'm still an activist*, no matter how concealed.

Having left California a black activist and Black Panther, I returned in 1990 on the tail end of a drug war. My parents' house in East Oakland was a stone's throw from the site of Felix Mitchell's notorious drug operation. There I sat, night after night, writing and listening to the sound track of urban warfare--gunshots, sirens, ambulances. I felt like I had been in exile in New Jersey for 18 years. Why, I asked myself, did I keep seeing the dark side of life itself, and even here, the underbelly of Cali? I came home to aging parents who shared how they had fought the sordid underbelly their whole time in Cali. I listened more closely than before I had left home to their tales of migration from Oklahoma, so like the Joads in Steinbeck's *Grapes of Wrath*.

In Oakland, my buried past surfaced. One night, I went to see a play about the Party that was so sensationalized I was horrified. I couldn't help it. I got up at the talk after the reading and spoke: "300 years from now, people won't realize how profoundly the Panthers transformed Oakland. Why do you think Oakland hasn't gone up in flames every time one of those riot epidemics sweeps the nation? The Panthers. But if this play has its way, all the world will know is that Bobby sold barbeque sauce, and Huey snorted coke."

I sat near Lake Merritt on a bright day. Why, I asked myself, do I keep seeing the dark side, the underbelly of California? The answers to that question have led me to the underbelly repeatedly.

Having left the state after being a black activist and Black Panther, I came back on the tail end of a magnificent drug war. My parents' house in East Oakland , a stone's throw from the site of Felix Mitchell's drug operation, was where I sat, night after night, writing and listening to the sound track of urban warfare--gunshots, sirens, ambulances. Perhaps, that's why I see the underbelly.

I'm the child of Oklahomans—perhaps another reason. My folks migrated in the 30s and 40s to escape segregation and fill wartime jobs. As a child I heard their stories as tall tales: Each relative arriving at the Santa Fe terminus in Berkeley shepherded from down south by kindly Pullman Porters. Saving down payments in Mason jars for homes even though Granddad was one of Oklahoma's first black oil millionaires. Dad a Tuskegee Airman, 332nd Fighter Group, saluting his CO, Benjamin O. Davis. Mom and Dad owning the only black taxicab company in the Eastbay in the 40s. My parents and other migrated blacks told to Go Home after the war.

I get that *Anti-vagabond* is one of my themes. I came home to my aging parents who, I finally gleaned, had fought the sordid underbelly their whole time in Cali. I have tremendous grief and appreciation for their generation.

The leakage from the underbelly kept happening in public and wholescale in my writing. By 2013, I was ready to come all the way out. I published my semi-autobiographical novel, opening myself to ridicule, criticism, scorn, praise, censure, acclaim, and applause, whatever. As a young person, I had no idea what I wanted to become, only knew that I wrote for every newspaper around me. To my astonishment, I became a witness to history, a scribe, and finally perhaps a griot. It took a while to grasp that witnessing is a process as unfathomable and deep as the oceans.

THE BLACK BODY, THE BLACK SKULL:
The natural as helmet

Similar to many black women maneuvering through history, I became a worker bee. In the BPP and the movemen, and at The Black House in the Fillmore district in San Francisco, I saw first hand the breakthrough of the color caste in the black community. The Black is Beautiful movement ended unhealthy limitations on physical appearance far more for black women than for black men.

How one wears the helmet of black hair is hotly debated in the black family and community. Appearance and success are intertwined in our population where Euro-centrism's prized paleness of skin, hair and eye color retains an oppressive hold, never more so than with black hair. Success in that crowning is a survival determinant. My several examples of black women manipulating African hair shows that we take our nappy hair and figure it out. Through trial and error, we have devised ways to fit in, challenge or adapt since we came to America as indentured servants centuries ago. We have been a part of the work force from jump street, in the fields, the big house, the marketplaces, sewing, cooking, planting, harvesting, often keeping our thick coiled hair under wrap. There were even Negro codes governing our dress and hair. South Carolina law required masters to clothe slaves in accord with the Negro Act of 1735. For the hair, sunbonnets; annual clothing distributions from plantation owners included palmetto hats and turbans, After Emancipation, West African women and African American women combined slave clothing and American styles.("Dress of The African American Woman in Slavery and Freedom: 1500 To 1935" Lydia Jean Wares)

My examples here are hair pioneer MADAME C. J. WALKER; my late friend and movie icon VONETTA MCGEE; newscaster

MELBA TOLLIVER; and the sisters of THE Black Panther Party. In each instance, the way our hair grew out of our scalp, its texture, was manipulated chemically, with heat, or with the barber's clippers to fit a prevailing societal requirement. To be able to earn one's keep, to be accepted by one's peers, one could not simply pull one's hair into a ponytail. One had to texturize, clip, press, shape, alter, or risk being fired, shunned, relegated, ostracized or ignored.

MADAME C. J. WALKER [1867-1919] invented "The Walker System" which was grooming to promote hair growth and condition the scalp using her shampoo, her pomade, strenuous brushing, and applying heated iron combs to the hair. She never claimed to have invented the hot comb. Mme. Walker widened the fingers of the comb and popularized it by refining it. By 1914. there was enormous competition, even hot comb wars, to address the market of black women who had to go to work.

I met Vonetta in 1967 when we were SF State students involved in the black theater scene in the Fillmore District in San Francisco. We became fast friends and stayed in contact until the end of her life. By 1974, Vonetta McGee THE MOVIE STAR was able to show in "Thomasine and Bushrod," an underrated film classic, the natural beauty and strength of an unadorned black woman of the plains as well as a sophisticated criminal. This film was produced and written by her then partner Max Julien. But she did her own hair, makeup and clothing, knowing exactly what she wanted to project.

Stills from the movie show her hair chemically untreated, her nappy edges showing. Max similarly wears the Afro.

In another still, Vonetta, Max and Gordon Parks Jr, the director of the film, are at work: she hasn't had to texturize, i.e. change her hair. In this film, at one point, Max's character, a bank robber, loses his nerve, and Vonetta's character slaps the shit out of him. This is an allusion to Harriet Tubman's famous warning to the escaped slaves who wanted to turn back during the difficult underground journey. Tubman said,"If you turn back, I'll shoot you."

Vonetta starred in "To Sleep With Anger," the film by Charles Burnett, another black-auteur. She is letting her edges, in this clip, show the way her hair grows naturally. She's not masquerading gelled down baby hair, which is the current fashion that is used to evoke a mixed racial heritage and trash the African heritage.. She was working with these unsung black directors who were conscious of the black cultural legacy they were building.

In a pr photo for "Blacula," she wears a short natural for the role she got after one of her several bouts with cancer. She had lost her hair to cancer treatments and told me that when it grew back she intended to never wear it short again. She didn't prefer it. But at the moment it served her well in her career.

In Clint Eastwood's "The Eiger Sanction," working for Hollywood studios, she was back to wigs. White actors wear wigs as a matter of course. However their wigs mimick the texture and shape of their natural hair. Black actors were required to have hair like whites, unlike their own, a form of cultural denial to put it lightly, oppression to give it a harsher name. This adherence to white hair styling also promulgated employment discrimination against black hair stylists who were nonentities in the industry. Those barriers are breaking down now.

In 1971, NEWSCASTER Melba Tolliver's hairdo, an Afro, got her fired from WABC-NY. [Here is her hairdo before the incident, and after.]

In an interview, she said, "The day before I was supposed to cover Tricia Nixon's wedding at the White House, I got my hair changed to a natural—previously, I'd been having it straightened—and can you believe they actually told me I couldn't appear live in the studio unless I changed my hair back to the way it used to look? They said I looked less attractive—less feminine. But it was their standard of femininity, not mine."

Tolliver refused to straighten her hair and as an ABC on-air talent, she was toast.

In the 1960s, in THE BLACK PANTHER PARTY, many women, including myself, wore the natural, the Afro, and were often photographed at rallies, protests and events. We braided it at night for length and sway. It had to be carefully shaped by barbers, and we patted it down each day before spraying to hold it in place.

A helmet is a form of protective gear worn to protect the head and the brain. The Afro was more than ceremonial or symbolic. It was akin to helmets worn by police, Hazmat workers, astronauts, pilots, worker facing dangerous conditions. The national, unprecedented hunt for Angela Davis after the prisoner escape and courthouse killings of George and Jonathan Jackson and others in 1970 in northern California showed this. The FBI put a whole nation on alert, giving permission to profile, harass and arrest black women with naturals.

Presently, the black lesbian community has taken the battle to new levels. Kinsey Clarke says: "In Black lesbian communities, cultural aesthetic standards are the driving force behind our signifiers: locs, fades, high-quality wigs and natural hairstyles [They] are [our] calling cards."

Thus the struggle and the use of black hair as a weapon in the fight for justice continues. The black woman historically has not been afraid of showing who she is ethnically. But she's had to be careful where and when to be courageous.

JUDY JUANITA

AN ARTIST-IN-PROGRESS

I was a fellow in the Robert Frierson Playwrighting Workshop at the Lorraine Hansberry Theatre (LHT) in San Francisco in 1991 where I learned golden lessons about myself and writing. By journaling, I understood that:

- **I learn through making big, fat mistakes vs. reading/ perfecting in my mind.**
- **The main trade secret I keep getting is that theatre is a closed shop but the one (other) entry is through perfected skill.**
- **My main reason for taking so many workshops is to keep writing.**
- **I'm trying to see where I should put my primary emphasis - poetry, fiction, or playwrighting.**
- **Oh boy, writers need support systems badly.**
- **Being mentored by extraordinary people is a strong theme in my work.**

Stanley, the head of LHT, came in the first night and spoke to the fellows. He shook the guys' hands and not mine. I was the only woman present. He seemed to avoid my eyes and couldn't remember my name. I seemed to recall this kind of chummy clique-y attitude in theater before. Circles are closed until you break through. Our "esteemed" playwright-leader Robert hardly talked about tonight's subject - plot and structure. Instead he sounded on how he hadn't gotten paid yet from LHT. When Stanley left, he dissed him. So, the men don't like him either…next week: there were two more women. What a relief. Stanley came in and ignored me again. He spoke to the other women…maybe he's not a misogynist…I noticed one thing about this workshop which was so hard to get in, so very very selective: it wasn't making me productive…Nina, the sculptor, and I talked a lot because we were always on time and Robert 1/2 hour late. I liked her. She was from the Midwest, like my college roomie. I love Midwesterners. I can connect with their dry humor. …Robert talked about the Henry Tanner play he was writing…I liked that he gave up a lot of information about the theater. He deglamorized it. When he got the SF Bay Guardian award, he was driving a cab--one cliché I never wanted to experience. Cleaning condos for two years was enough for my bones. Robert and my previous playwrighting instructor quoted Lagos Egri like his book was the Bible. I read it but it was hard for me to grasp.

I learn through doing and making mistakes vs. reading and perfecting in my mind…Finally they got to my play. I'd been so selfish and self-absorbed. I only read Nina's and Mike's…The plays by Susan and Nate, the other two, I couldn't read with great interest; I picked them up and put them down unaffected. I missed class (flu) when they did Susan's. I liked her and would have hated to comment on her work…She'd been kicking around in costume design for 10 years professionally. She was from Spelman College, the Vassar of the Black colleges. She wanted to be called by Hollywood and make some dough instead of the $300 budget from Stanley. Did anybody like this guy? I got tons of suggestions - really explicit - on my play. Once home, I saw that Nate hated it. That hurt. I took his copy out the next day and studied it. Next class, he said, "I have real problems with this play," but said he had written them down and it wasn't necessary to go over them twice. Everybody's eyebrows rose. He didn't like the play or me…Philip Kan Gotunda was our guest playwright. Boy, was he interesting. A real careerist in a laid-back, surefooted way. Talk about being right person, right place, right time for Asian work. He was the one. Interesting to hear him and Robert talk about L.A. Theatre scene…so much is dependent on knowing the right person who likes your work/you. The chummies. On balance, this workshop was more discouraging than not.

The main trade secret I keep getting is that theatre is a closed shop but that the one entry is through perfected skill. We went for drinks, all of us, afterward. That helped; liquor loosens things. Philip spoke bluntly about being a token; let's not fool ourselves, he said. The conversation got a bit tight as Philip revealed he'd gotten some of that screenwriting money that Robert was always talking about. So many branches in the writing world, I don't know where to perch. Seems like a man's world to me - maybe that's why the fem/lesbians decided to go off and do their own thing.

My main reason for taking so many workshops is to keep writing. But my strategy didn't work with LHT; I needed feedback, not just weekly schmoozing. If I'm writing 20-page chapters for the novel or six-page scenes, I'm happy. If not, I'm not...I went to see Robert's play at The Herbst. The Abe Lincoln Brigade, old line Berkeley radicals of the folk singing variety, filled the place for a benefit. It was like a step back in time with the play being *Uncle Tom's Cabin* in modernist take. It was interesting. Very clumsily-acted in parts. I sat behind Robert. The play was stridently polemical, melodramatic, but it worked. I determined to learn how to use melodrama. I didn't want to write a thinky play. Robert grumbled that the Tanner play only had one technical run through. He was pissed at Stanley for that. He said two checks from the SF Mime Troupe bounced also. I got a negative sensation in my gut. He'd been doing this shtick, winning prizes, getting plays on the black experience mounted since 1979 but seemed stuck on a career ladder with the waning black theater vogue. Was this where I was headed? Bounced checks and writing plays for silver-haired radicals?

I'm really trying to see where I should put my primary emphasis--poetry, fiction, or playwrighting. I'm not young; I had to make some decisions at this intersection. Writing had been a delicious buffet as I sampled poetry, fiction and playwriting. I needed to "go all the way" with one but wondered if I could. Was I just a big enthusiast with varied talents? Robert was doing a play on Huey P. Newton and the party. Since I was a Panther and we'd talked about it before, he wanted to pick my brains. "I wasn't in on the big stuff. I was behind-the-scenes." *I'm picking my own brains, Buster. Go find another brain to pick.* I felt like I'd never get anything of substance from him - and I liked him. He was funny and touching but struggling just like I was. Only he'd had umpteen productions. What's it all about, Alfie?

Oh boy, writers need support systems badly. I worked hard and brought in a scene. Robert was remodeling his house (money must've been coming in from somewhere) and was so busy all he did was jaw on the remodel. Somebody else would've called this sexist, that he always had his own concerns primary. And there was a sexual undercurrent between us that I tried to ignore. I heard LHT had to almost shut down, and maybe wouldn't have the readings at all. Strangely, this was a relief. Did I need a reading under these circumstances? *Why aren't I more enthusiastic about this reading? For starters, how about—I have some standards of my own. I'm not just a fish out here to be flipped around.* As things began to wrap on the fellowship, I was trying to think positive and put playwrighting in a proper perspective. What did I get? What did I lose? I went to the last workshop out of sorts. Too many balls juggling my othermanuscripts; and again, was I going to have to choose between fiction, poetry and playwriting? I made a big flub and forgot the main character in someone's play. The writer looked at me, aghast, then quickly recouped and the conversation went on.

Burn out. From there on out, I was fishing in the jumble inside me. I needed renewal. I'd lost motivation. I was getting sick. LHT called to say the readings were on. The manuscript was not done. It was hard to rev back up. I called LHT. Got my deadline extended. When the staged reading did go up, it was—surprise, surprise— well-attended, 60+ people. A lively discussion. I waited for a nibble, a crumb, anything—for weeks. Stanley called—the play would go forward. He gave me a date. Sure enough, my play, my very own play, got advance mention in *The San Francisco Chronicle* Datebook. It felt real. At my next meeting with Stanley, I brought up payment, compensation, moolah. He said the budget was tight, tight, tight. "But I will be paid something?" He jumped up from the table and threw my precious script down, getting loud and funky. "I made Ntozake Shange. How dare you question me!" I yelled back, "You have to pay me something. What are you saying? Not even my carfare from across the Bay." He stormed out. I didn't know what to think except crazy. Two days later, he left a phone message: LHT was pulling the production because of lack of funds. I went back to the novel, a coming-of-age story.

Ironically **being mentored by extraordinary people is a strong theme in my work.** I have been exposed to a colorful lot of male writers and artists, putative fathers who showed me their discipline and craft. I absorbed my lessons while assisting, chauffeuring, transcribing, interviewing, opening for, cleaning house or buying groceries for The Artist, witnessing all manner of excess, alcoholics, egomaniacs, dissolutes, self-centered pricks, fame hounds, leeches, misogynists, stuffed shirts, wife abusers and serial adulterers.

Because of that exposure I kept the idea of a full-fledged artistic career at arms length for many years. I thought that the horrid qualities invariably came with great and even not-so-great accomplishment. The successful women artists I encountered were hardworking, self-sacrificing, generous, often defiantly unhappy and did their own shitwork. Although they seemed to be happier once they achieved a certain level of success and financial independence, I concluded early on that being an artist was damaging to one's own life and to loved ones. Reading about the writers of the Harlem Renaissance, watching and reading Beat and post-Beat writers, befriending the writers of the black arts movement in the 1960s/70s, I repressed my artistic ambitions - fascinated, terrified, humbled by their commitment and passion, horrified by the sacrifice, chaos and suffering of their loved ones.

Perhaps I was simply an impressionable young person. I had come, after all, from a strict religious family. The imbalance in my family of origin, my mother, in my mind, turning whole-hog to religion as a salve for my father's compulsive gambling, triggered my susceptibility to being disillusioned by any pseudo-parents. It took a while to find the parent in myself, to paraphrase Ntozake Shange's

For Colored Girls Who Have Considered Suicide When the Rainbow Was Enuf ("I found God in myself"). It took time to acquire the wisdom that experience brings. Once I got it, I understood how to live a balanced life <u>and</u> pursue writing.

CLEANING OTHER PEOPLE'S HOUSES

When a friend asked me to join her condominium-cleaning business in my 40s, I recoiled. Moi? A black woman with degrees, fellowships, travels abroad, a library of dictionaries within my library - a cleaning woman? Cleaning other people's houses was necessity to my grandmothers, anathema to my mother and history to me. Was she out of her mind?

For certain black women, the Task is laid out early: get a good education, a good job; don't let any man bring you down; and don't look back. We're marched into society like toy soldiers to uphold the virtue of the race. When the mechanism runs down, the well-meaning elders who equipped us with our weapons of education, enunciation and etiquette are often several cities away.

Out of work, out of gas, going through a hellified midlife crisis, I had wearied of the Task. But, even in a breach, I was not supposed to clean toilets for a living. Loaded down with clients, my friend, a resilient, red-haired, onetime hippie, asked again. She and I had burned out as teachers. My funds narrowing, I accepted with a barrage of provisos: just for a while…just to see what it was like… until something better comes along.

For the next twenty months, we cleaned pricey condos in suburban New Jersey, luxury Siamese boxes with a sameness of design that made cleaning a matter of tactile geometry. My dismayed girlfriends, journalists and teachers all, suggested I incorporate, set up an agency for cleaning women, be a supplier of labor, not, for heaven's sake, the laborer herself. I had even written about domestics, paying homage from the safe distance of poetry: *the last maid in my line my grandmother young/a chambermaid in a Muskogee hotel gingerly/picked up soiled towels shielding the pupils/of her young eyes from couples coupling uncoupling/requesting fresh white towels her daughter told/me this young/teaching me to read and read well/so I'd never have this to fall back on.*

Nevertheless, some fundamental, driving curiosity, and necessity, wouldn't let up. I fell back on it. The daughter who had been spared housework to do homework found cleaning other people's houses full of goalposts and tasks, the completion of which yielded immediate benefits. Shine, freshness, order and tranquility displaced metaphors, sestinas, end rhymes and point of view.

The experience had an adolescent tinge to it. With the music blasting and time sliding by in four-hour, eighty-dollar blocks, the money piled up. As in adolescence, the goal was speed. Finish a condo, do a second, eat Tex-Mex, do a third. I learned shortcuts for every possible household chore.

Bathrooms and kitchens were singularly important. Clients looked there to see their money's worth. Getting the showers clean was sloppy at first. Standing on rags and towels, we applied fabric softener (less toxic), rinsed it off, dried the surround, and ended up sopping wet. Finally, we figured if we cleaned the shower in t he buff, our clothes would stay dry and we wouldn't use up rags which we laundered. Of course, one day, our psychiatrist-client came home early. Marvin Gaye was blasting, the water was running, the doctor was in his bedroom before I knew it. I hollered, "Don't come in!" When I came out, I let him know exactly how we got his glass shower to sparkle. He seemed amused.

Typically, our mostly male clients never saw us. Bachelors, divorced men, gay couples, widowers, they left early or were away on business for days at a time. I liked cleaning their houses, polishing their mirrors, turning on t heir superior sound systems, and dusting and bopping my way through their cool environments. Instead of the forced voyeurism I had heard about, I discovered an inverted voyeurism, an intimacy minus the intimate. I was inside their lives; their lives were inside mine. I knew which deodorant they used, which sections of the paper they treasured, the radio stations they listened to, the real color of their hair, the amount of liquor they consumed, their taste in books.

I found these forays into the male domain like simulated wife maneuvers. It should have been no surprise that I had more problems with women, especially those who had difficulty relinquishing dominion. There were those who couldn't leave the room, let alone the house, while we were in it. Those didn't last long. One woman had her toddler present me with the day's pay, crumpled and sweaty. The second time it happened, I told her it was demeaning. Although she apologized, that was the end of that. We had more business than we could handle.

I think it was harder for women to pay for a service they traditionally provided free, as an unspoken stipulation of the marriage contract. It was also harder for some women clients to accept that their houses needed extra cleaning, i.e. extra money, whereas the men wanted the work done and use us out of there when they got home…period.

The home of an interracial, professional gay couple was my favorite. The black man, Ron, had an arresting blow-up of his grandfather upstairs; its piercing eyes followed me as I dusted and vacuumed. I found myself asking his portrait questions, giving rejoinders, packing whole histories of my life into twenty-minute conversations.

One week, I couldn't help notice a book about AIDS on the nightstand. As weeks went by, more books appeared. My friend and I speculated over lunch as to which one was sick. It didn't take long to discover that Ron was in an advanced stage. I got used to his being home, the clink of his spoon as he ate ice cream, the way he padded from room to room as we cleaned, switching on cable news.

The grandfather's gaze encompassed my feelings, an array that surfaced involuntarily as the illness progressed. I felt reproach, anger, sorrow, anguish. One day, I came downstairs, my "dialogue" finished for the day. I walked into the living room and recognized instantly the two women there as Ron's mother and sister. Their physical similarity to the gruff grandfather was softened by their protective stances. We stood there, a strange familiarity between us, this gay man, his family and me. Little in our upbringing had given us sight of these eventualities, that he would be openly gay, that they would be supportive as he died of AIDS, that I would be his Beulah.

Whenever I ran into problems, cleaning or otherwise, I fell back on the great rhetorical "Why am I here?" Testing my strength against that of my ancestors? Tackling a horrific job that no one should ever have to do? I knew it was temporary, and it wasn't horrific, just tedious and inglorious.

One afternoon, a wife of a cardiologist was reduced to tears because a neighbor had snubbed her. Politely I offered sympathy, but I thought her sheltered, self-absorbed, spoiled. She constantly offered me lunch. I refused. I was intent on finishing her three-story townhouse in six hours. She offered more money because her place was larger. I accepted. Gradually we got to know each other, shared experiences in mothering, growing up, romance, grad school. It turned out we were both doctoral dropouts. I found out she was a wonderful cook; she learned I had read at her YWHA and asked to see my poetry. When she cried again, I could not dismiss her tears as trivial. I could no longer dismiss her point of view or her frame of reference.

I have never looked at myself as much as I did during those months of cleaning. Mirrors were everywhere. I began to see my life clearly, even starkly. In a pique, I quit one week and found work as an office temp at one-third the pay. The supervisor kept calling me Bertha ("I'm sorry, you look like a Bertha.") I stuck it out for four days before heading back to condo country where nobody called me Bertha, Beulah or Bessie.

I found out how strong I was, mentally and physically, after all those hours of bending, squatting, twisting, elbowing, polishing and emptying. However strong a mind I possessed, though, my body couldn't take it. My back, always strong, began to ache.

One morning, a fiftyish matron insisted that we sit and discuss *The Color Purple* which she had just finished reading. We talked about the horror and beauty in Alice Walker's vision. The irony of our discussion didn't escape me. Alice Walker had championed Zora Neale Hurston, the novelist-folklorist of the Harlem Renaissance who had spent her last impoverished decade as a domestic in Florida.

I didn't last much longer. The experiment was over.

Not long after, I passed a woman, black like me, carrying her plastic bags into a subdivision lined with three-story colonials. I felt a mixture of empathy, relief and gratitude. With no alternative choices or yuppie townhouses to "lite" clean, I suspect her working conditions were much harsher than mine had been. Cleaning other people's houses was her necessity, and, for a time, it had been my necessity too. Doing her job helped me cross the threshold of middle-age. Cleaning other people's houses had made my own life habitable again.

WHATEVER HAPPENED TO CAROLYN M. RODGERS?

There couldn't have been more than six people in the large auditorium of the Fruitvale Branch library in East Oakland, circa 1994. The poet, Carolyn M. Rodgers, read her work to the interested handful, her voice echoing in the empty auditorium. I was mortified at the turnout for this icon of the black poetry movement .Why weren't there more poetry lovers? They'd had ample notice. True, she wasn't a supernova like Sonia Sanchez or Angela Davis, though she had nine books of poetry. After a flurry of fame in the sixties, she had become the phantom of the Black Arts Movement (BAM), disappearing for decades at a clip before resurfacing in her beloved Oakland, California or her native Chicago. When we went out to dinner after the reading, she told me being a poet was about champagne or beer, i.e. speaking before thousands or a few, with something precious in every encounter. We exchanged e-mails when she returned to Chicago. http://aalbc.com/authors/carolyn-rodgers.html

Mar 3, 2005

I don't guess I ever told you about the time I was asked to speak at SIU (Southern Illinois University). It's a big campus here in Illinois, and carries a lot of prestige here in the state. The black students had just been given a new campus house for their functions and they had named it after Gwendolyn Brooks. I was very excited about going there to read my poetry. The letter stated that I would receive $450, plus traveling and eating expenses. Not bad. So I went. Not one single student showed up for the reading! Not one! The first and last time it ever happened to me! They made some lame excuse and said that students were probably busy studying for finals. I was given my check (glory, glory) and I took my wounded pride home. Several days later, I received a letter saying that they were sorry that I had not been paid (!) and they sent me a second check. An obvious mistake! It doesn't get much better than that. It doesn't get much worse than that by this I mean no one showing up!

Things will get better, I'm sure. You learn from it all. Hopefully, one day we will look back and laugh at it all!

Hang tough! Luv Ya!
Carolyn

The main event in her public life was her emergence and dominant role in the Black Arts Movement. It would define her life. In 1967, she partnered with fellow poets Don L. Lee-Haki Madhubuti and Johari Amini to found Third World Press (TWP). Thus began one of the Black Arts Movement's most successful presses on a mimeo machine in a basement apartment on Chicago's South Side. Rodgers, a Chicago native born in 1940, earned her BA from Roosevelt University in 1965 and would complete her M.A. in English from the University of Chicago in 1980. A central *padnuh* in the OBAC (Organization of Black American Culture) coterie, she prospered as it flourished. TWP published her first book, <u>Paper Soul</u>. Hoyt Fuller, editor of *Negro Digest/Black World*, wrote the introduction. Her footpath in the poetry world followed the standard operating procedure for artists – initial emergence within a clique, break with the clique or clique dissolves, fade to black or transcend. *Umbra*, the Lower East Side collective put Ishmael Reed, David Henderson, and Steve Cannon and Calvin C. Hernton on the map. The beats gave LeRoi Jones-Amiri Baraka his lift-off; The Journal of Black Dialogue

David Peñalosa explores the roots of it all in *The Clave Matrix- Afro-Cuban Rhythm: Its Principles and African Origins.*

in San Francisco put Marvin X in orbit. The essential difference in Chicago was the presence of a woman mentor, Gwendolyn Brooks, a writer of stature. Rodgers wasn't Brooks' mistress, wife, maidservant, fuckbuddy or sycophant.

Feb 19, 2005

...I found one of my old essays where I was using the f-word all over the place! Now I know what they liked about me. I had forgotten me. I was almost completely irreverent at times, and might I say with gusto and a flair! I couldn't believe who I was. It was real food for thought. No wonder they look at me the way they do now! I still believe that half the battle though in getting published is who you know. I was very lucky to be in Chicago with Gwendolyn Brooks and many famous literary people came to sit at her table and I met them. I believe though that you have to keep on putting yourself out there. That's what I have to do, otherwise I am an interesting artifact. Or as I told some of my students, I'm history, literally.

Keep the faith. I love the sunshine and laughter you keep sending. My days are getting brighter. Definitely! Hope yours are too.

Standing in that East Oakland library auditorium, her head wrapped in African cloth, Rodgers read old poems and recent ones. Her newer work relied on biblical references, and on salt as a metaphor. "Throwing Salt" begins with the subtitle "Teshuva: To Balance the Scales." Teshuva is Hebrew for turning back to God.

"Since we use the/good in our past/to lead us to future good/ to remind us of what man is capable/of, it seems/right then that we/ should use the evil/in our past also/to remind us of what man/is capable of."

That's her first stanza—proposition, theme, contention. The next line renders solution: "Salt is what/ it all becomes…" and later in the 26-line poem, a rueful observation: "The main event in life is something/We think we can plan, but can't…"

Rodgers' foremothers were Pulitzer Prize-winners Gwendolyn Brooks and Margaret Walker. Each was married, middle-aged, their work and social activism having surfaced in the 1930s-40s. Gwendolyn Brooks, in 1968, said:

> "There's something very special happening in poetry today and I see it happening chiefly among the young blacks. I think that later they will take out some of the unruly roughness, but right now, I'm just glad to see it coming out. I think after all of the activity there will be an intense interest in saying things more effectively, using language more effectively." Hopefully something will have been decided, and the poets will then have time to play more with their art."[1]

The movement for civil rights, like the abolitionist movement 100+ years earlier, gained traction once the world took notice. Once Europeans, especially the British, saw the horror and treachery of slavery from abolitionists, slave narratives and ex-slaves travelling abroad, emancipation was foreseeable. President John F. Kennedy had proffered a tepid response to the Emancipation Proclamation's 100th anniversary until pressured by civil rights activists to approve the March on Washington.[2] The American workforce was changing as were TV, radio, pop records, magazines, fashion. Rhythm and Blues (R&B) was the persistent beat undercutting that. The Cuban

---

1   A Life of Gwendolyn Brooks, George E. Kent. University Press of Kentucky (2009) 228.

2   "The Kennedys were almost morbidly afraid of this march. They understood there'd been nothing like it," said Rep. Eleanor Holmes Norton, D-District of Columbia, who helped plan the march 50 years ago. http://www.cnn.com/2013/08/28/politics/march-on-washington-kennedy-jitters/index.html

embargo cut off Americans from the overt knowledge of the Cuban influence on music, especially R&B. Bo Diddley had fused a 3-2 clave with rhythm and blues, and rock and roll. A Bo Diddley beat meant a clave-based motif. Clave is the name of the patterns played on two hardwood sticks in Afro-Cuban music ensembles.[3] This syncopated accent on the "off beat" was perfect for the click-and-slip of the pelvis in many popular dances of the time, including the boogaloo, shimmy, Hully Gully, Hitch Hike, Popcorn, Jerk, Philly Dog. Watusi, to name a few. BAM poets, the predecessors of hip hop and rap, were the Bo Diddleys of the poetry world, working the off beat as hard as they could, jerking, shimmying, boogalooing, popcorning, jerking and philly dogging in all the urban hot spots.

> Feb 12, 2005
>
> I was most appreciative of the interview that you sent me. Ossie Davis & Ruby Dee have been friends of mine for a long time! Years ago, Ruby came to Chicago to do a reading and she was using one of my poems. She asked if anyone knew how to get in contact with me. She thought I might like to see the performance. Hence, the beginning of a long friendship. I was in Walgreen's buying some stuff and the Black salesgirl, (a young girl) told me [about Ossie Davis' passing]. I knew then that he had indeed left an indelible and lasting mark. She was barely twenty and she was saddened by his passing. I was overwhelmed, right there in the store. But in my life, that's how things are right now. We all have this curtain call. And I'm busy living and trying to love my life as much as possible, hoping I get it all together and have plenty of time to do it! I want to teach five classes in one class. Happy Valentine's Day!

In "The Last M.F." Rodgers defends her use of profanity by vowing to not use it, but to be, "as the new Black Womanhood suggests/a softer self…" Then, signaling she—a modern, intelligent, educated, outspoken sistah for the ages—won't be silenced, she writes "...I only call muthafuckas, muthafuckas/so no one should be insulted."

Jan 6, 2006

I was thinking about you and the new year and hoping that this will be my year to win the metaphorical lottery and get back to Oakland! I long to see Oakland. It's like my second home. I was just telling my friend who lives there and was born and raised here that I envy her so much. I fear flying. That's my problem. I am hoping to psyche myself out of it this year. I'd be in and out, just like that!

As for the burst pipes and my storage...I just went through the most difficult thing I've encountered in life. My black book collection, my letters from Margaret Walker, Ruby Dee & Ossie, Gwendolyn Brooks and stuff from Johnson Publishing Company was all but totaled...I had already willed my black book collection from the sixties, seventies and eighties to the Black Student Organization at the University of Chicago. I've actually got to change my will. I have no black book collection, anymore... Some of the anthologies I was published in, about thirty, all perished. My contributor's copies. But enough already. This WAS a lesson in detachment. I DID think about what it might have felt like if instead of a storage space, it had been my HOME. So, life goes on and we pick up the pieces, such as they are, and we are grateful for sunny and even rainy days.

Happy New Year. Let's try to fulfill some of our dreams this year. In spite of all that went down in 2005, I cannot honestly say that it was my worst year. It really wasn't. Tuesday, I go to find out if this stomach tumor has shrunk any after three months of medical therapy. Chant for me, please... Peace out.

In her work, she utilized language as a weapon to draw attention to larger social issues in an era that was an amalgam of social change. The Beatles invaded the U.S. and celebrated their R&B roots. Women were leaving home and pink ghettos. Civil rights legislation forced corporations and retailers business to disregard in contemporary music. Stroffolino contends that the incessant demands of commerce in a capitalist society prevent the authentic, the spontaneous. The BAM was perhaps the last time the noncommercial expression of black dialogue, the black aural expression, surfaced, the last time it was representable. By the end of the black-is-beautiful phase, blackness was commodified. Integration meant not only school busing and affirmative action, but Diahann Carroll in *Julia* on TV, all gussied up and proper, her single parenthood in Claudine transmogrified to a lunch-pail, and antiseptic widowhood which conferred respectability (unlike Carroll's 1972 Oscar-nominated character in Claudine who had six kids out-of-wedlock).

Jan 17, 2008

...I have been corresponding for at least two years, probably more, with a PH.D. Black history professor at the ______. He was writing a book, his third or fourth to be published, and he wrote me about using some of my work and that's how it started. Through my illness and madness and everything, he was right there. Well, I hadn't heard from him for a few weeks, and I'd sent him a Christmas card. I thought it odd that I hadn't heard from him but he was the Chairperson of the African-American/Black Studies Department there, so he was very very busy, at times. Well last week I got the card back. A note was scribbled on it, which simply said "sorry, deceased." I almost fainted. What? He was 62 years old and happily planning his retirement!!! I couldn't believe it!

So I called the school and his secretary told me that he had slipped and he fell and fractured his skull in the parking lot when he was keeping a doctor's appointment! And that was it... I am a changed woman. Life keeps making me change, just when I think I can handle it all or it's all okay or this or that, something happens. He had been teaching for 34 years and was looking forward to retiring. He's written 7 books and had 3 more coming. It scared me. It intimidated me...And to make matters worse here, the sun has all but abandoned Chicago. For days on end we are overcast. It is gloomy, and dark, many days, one right after the other. We all have SAD, Seasonal Affective Disorder, and today it is just almost 3 o'clock and it's almost dark. It's too much! For this cause, in 1986, I left Chicago and first moved to Oakland.

What's happening on your end of the world? We're holding fort here.

In "Salt: Prospective," Rodgers wrote about her concept of God:
What emerged was the philosopher poet exploring the human condition, while nodding benevolently at contraries, yet no longer at war with the status quo.

Her lyric heart cries its independence in the midst of anxiety, in the conflict between the necessity of hardness and the ideal of feminine softness: "...knowing the music of/silence/hating it/ hoarding it/loving it/treasuring it,/it often birthing our creativity/we are lonely/ being soft and being hard/supporting our selves, earning/ our own bread/soft/hard/hard/soft/knowing that need must not/ show..."

Unlike Tyler Perry's Madea, who's become a head-snapping, celluloid Sapphire-in-perpetuity, anguish, bewilderment <u>and</u> audacity are a big part of the Rodgers early poetic persona. She was able to express the pain of being a black woman in a society that found such beings at distinct odds with its definition of femininity: "I went through my/Mean period/If you remember/I spit/out nails/ Chewed tobacco on/The paper/And dipped some bad snuff..."

But the pain changes two stanzas later: "...I woke up one/ Morning/And looked at myself/And what I saw was/Carolyn/Not imani ma jua or soul/Sistah poetess of/The moment/I saw a woman. Human and/Black.

Nov. 9, 2004

I am just hanging on here. In Chicago, people are pretty
sobered after the election and blame is going everywhere. I
had to have oral surgery Saturday and I have stitches in my
mouth, so I'm not debating anybody about anything much!

I went to my second conference though yesterday, for
women who want to start their own business. It was held
at the Hyatt Hotel here and I had been planning to attend
for months; I wasn't about to stay home because of my
mouth. I'm so glad I went. It was all about woman power!
Women of every race, creed, and color, (to borrow a cliché)
were there, and we were all trying to break the glass ceiling,
among other things. I wouldn't have missed it for the world.

I would like to learn how to create a web site. I am hoping
that when I do go back to teach it will only be for a short
time. But who knows? I might get a real good [book]
deal, anyway, as we settle in, for what lies ahead. Thanks
for putting me on your mailing list. There is so much good
head food that you send me. Sometimes, I am awed by
people's capacity to still articulate in extremely erudite, yet
down-to-earth fashion, the challenges that we face today.
Everybody here was overjoyed that Barack Obama/
won over Alan Keyes. I'm guessing that you know who
those two are.

The Black community here though is still quite stunned
and Jesse Jackson held a historic meeting with Minister
Farrakhan and they talked about what our new challenges
are. People were invited to comment and it was all very
good and helpful. So, life goes on...Keep the faith! Chant
some good things for me and I will affirm good things
for you!!! Singer-songwriter-poet Chris Stroffolino, aka
Piano Van Man, bemoans the loss of the representable

in contemporary music.[4] Stroffolino contends that the incessant demands of commerce in a capitalist society prevent the authentic, the spontaneous. The BAM was perhaps the last time the noncommercial expression of black dialogue, the black aural expression, surfaced, the last time it was representable. By the end of the black-is-beautiful phase, blackness was commodified. Integration meant not only school busing and affirmative action, but Diahann Carroll in "Julia" on TV, all gussied up and proper, her single parenthood in *Claudine* transmogrified to a lunch-pail, and antiseptic widowhood which conferred respectability (unlike Carroll's 1972 Oscar-nominated character in *Claudine* who had six kids out-of-wedlock).

Jan 17, 2008

… I have been corresponding for at least two years, probably more, with a PH.D. Black history professor at the ______. He was writing a book, his third or fourth to be published, and he wrote me about using some of my work and that's how it started. Through my illness and madness and everything, he was right there. Well, I hadn't heard from him for a few weeks, and I'd sent him a Christmas card. I thought it odd that I hadn't heard from him but he was the Chairperson of the African -American/Black Studies Department there, so he was very very busy, at times. Well last week I got the card back. A note was scribbled on it, which simply said "sorry, deceased." I almost fainted. What? He was 62 years old and happily planning his retirement!!! I couldn't believe it!

So I called the school and his secretary told me that he had slipped and he fell and fractured his skull in the parking lot when he was keeping a doctor's appointment! And that was it... I am a changed woman. Life keeps making me change, just

[4] http://chris-stroffolino.tumblr.com/post/102613873124/03-life-in-a-tin-can

when I think I can handle it all or it's all okay or this or that, something happens. He had been teaching for 34 years and was looking forward to retiring. He's written 7 books and had 3 more coming. It scared me. It intimidated me….And to make matters worse here, the sun has all but abandoned Chicago. For days on end we are overcast. It is gloomy, and dark, many days, one right after the other. We all have SAD, Seasonal Affective Disorder, and today it is just almost 3 o'clock and it's almost dark. It's too much! For this cause, in 1986, I left Chicago and first moved to Oakland.

What's happening on your end of the world? We're holding fort here.

From the cradle up our grannies, aunties, mommas taught what I call The Black Woman's National Anthem: you can do bad by yo-self. Taking this maxim to heart while embracing the open sexuality and unbridled militancy of the era, Rodgers, Sonia Sanchez, et al, and their entry into publication and the reading circuit brought a new artistic voice into the poetry community. With their parallels to R&B, their uncommon voices crossed genres and traduced boundaries, mixed slang, nostalgia, curse words and sociological analysis, utilizing:

- direct speech and direct address,
- frank hope, frank distress
- sexual pleas for attention and raw revelation, sexual intimacies
- explicit language
- confessionals that evoked anger v. pity

The poems were manifestoes of blatant and obscene phraseology: we will not disavow one another. We are significant not insignificant. We stand in unity to avert disaster. The white woman can spit in her man's face (and 40 years later lean in). But we stand with you, brother. They addressed the abyss between black men and women by looking at it and acknowledging its presence as problematic issue in the community. This new work located the black community, despite dispersion due to migration, mobility and integration. Its black heart was the community unlike traditional poetry. Thus it transgressed the norms with obscene image of the black heart, the black pudenda, black desire. Thomas Kuhn, the scientific philosopher who brought paradigm *shift* into the lexicon, said that intellectual courage is even rarer than physical courage. "Kuhn pointed out that ….an intellectually courageous person is willing to look at things that are surprisingly hard to look at" (David Brooks, NYT 8.28.14).

The new paradigm had its raison d'etre, its formalisms:
- natural hair v. hotcombed/chemical treated hair
- fierceness v. accommodation
- softness v. hardness
- Godlessness v. God-fearing
- Being colorful v. trying to blend in
- Black v. Negro
- Sympathy v. empathy. If you were angered by the poet's voice, you were perceiving inside the boundaries. If you pitied the poet's voice, you were outside the boundaries.

But as the BAM grew from rawness to maturation, paradigm shifts occurred in the religion of blackness, during and immediately after its establishment. Feminists and black lesbians contributed womanist to the dialogue. Offspring generations sampled rhythm and blues, thus reducing it to "the mix. Carolyn M. Rodgers reconverted to her Christian faith, having set God aside during her militant phase. Novelist Muriel Spark in "The Informed Air" reflects on the stresses of Job. "With God we have none of us any privacy, in itself an almost intolerable burden. If we did not set God aside in our minds for most of the time, we would be semi-paralyzed. We could never get anything done, never be ourselves."

Poets who emerged later, in the 70s and after, included Ntozake Shange, the late greats Lucille Clifton, Jayne Cortez and Wanda

Coleman, by turn fierce wise and soft. The stance, the growl, the ferocity of the black arts movement poems had startled me as much as a Black orthodoxy felt restrictive. The recently-deceased Wanda Coleman and I were born the same year, 1946. I had the privilege of meeting her at a good friend's dinner, although her crude insults thrown in our hostess' face offended me. I wondered, while reading her obituary, if the poetic personas many black poets adopted were a professional necessity. Did they, like Tupac and Biggie, gangsterize their public image to match the simmering rage of being black and oppressed in America? Graciousness was not a part of the black arts orthodoxy.

By embracing Christianity graciously in her writing, Carolyn became a heretic and an ecumenicist, in her characteristic embracing of opposites. When a radical friend trashed me for embracing Buddhism, Carolyn M. Rodgers wrote "Ten Worlds" which melds Buddhism and Christianity: "my Buddhist friend/tells me there are ten worlds...ten cesspools of sin?/or ten sanctuaries and gateways to heaven(s)/ten gardens of eden or/ten paths to travel...ten ways to laugh or cry and find or be found in....in the room of this house/I am catholic and I drink the blood, and eat the body of the lamb/god/ man/called Christ while my friend/chants in another/room of the house/ Nam-myoho-renge-kyo."

This is some distance from the angst and loneliness of her sixties classic, "Poem for Some Black Women " which expresses the dilemma of black women: i am lonely,/all the people i know/i know too well/there was comfort in that/at first but now/we know each other's miseries/too well...we are/lonely women, who spend/ time waiting for/occasional flings....we understand the world/ problems/Black women's problems with/Black men/but all/we really understand is/lonely..."

Sept 27, 2004

I just got your piece from E.L. Doctorow. It sorta blew me away! I just pulled it down/printed it out, and it made me want to write my own poem about the war and everything. I haven't finished reading the piece yet, but I wanted to respond quickly. Sometimes, it takes days for me to get to my e-mail. I don't do anything except work since I quit work! I can't believe I have even less time, but it almost seems that way.

I miss my job. And more than anything else, I miss getting paid every two weeks, even if it was almost slave labor. But the weather in Chicago in autumn is unbelievably beautiful, so I'm enjoying that. Especially, since it definitely isn't going to last. Maya Angelou was in our city tonight for a book signing. More to come. I'm just a rambling rose right now.

Yet Sonia Sanchez commented recently on the tempering of her work: "You must remember, in the time that we were writing, all the death and dying that happened and how we had discovered how much we'd been enslaved in this country…We came out hitting and slapping and alerting people to what had happened" (The Writer's Chronicle, Feb. 2014:29).

April 5, 2005

I am finally making some headway. And I don't mind telling you that your emails give me much motivation. I'm not just out here, "all by myself" trying to make it work/or happen! In the last two months I have bought 3 different pieces of software to do chapbooks with. Finally, it looks like one of them is going to work! It is actually viable, and I have been able to begin a decent dummy again. Glory, glory! Smile.

You are the playwright that I still want to be! I can't get to my plays yet at all. Too much going on around me… I don't know anymore how I had time to work! I will have to make drastic changes for this upcoming job in the fall. It's a seminar on older Black writers, like G. Brooks, Margaret Walker, Langston Hughes, Richard Wright, e al...So, life goes on.

Although she did fly under the radar in middle-age, her work and Sonia Sanchez's poetry furnished several generations with new paradigms and language. Influenced by E.E.Cummings' idiosyncratic grammar and punctuation, Rodgers and Sanchez, alongside Baraka, led the assault on tradition, transforming the Coleridge's "infinite I am" to "i am" and using repetition and alliteration to exploit cliché. When news becomes noose, meaning enlarges; calling the telephone cord "the witch cord/that erases the stretch of/thirty-three blocks/ and tuning in the voice which/woodenly stated that the/talk box was 'disconnected'..." critiques AT&T and monopoly capitalism; calling her mom "religious-negro" who is "religiously girdled in/her god..." is critique minus bitterness ("It's Deep: don't never forget the bridge that you crossed over on). Carolyn soldiered on through the times, anthologized many times over, appearing in *Essence* and *O* magazines, speaking locally.

> May 19, 2005
> Hey girl, I just had to share the good news. After not receiving any royalty statements from Doubleday for the last three years, I figured the little glory ride was over! But lo and behold (!), what was in my P.O. Box but a statement with a small check, after three long years. It made my day, possibly my year! Smile. Now all I need is a little more macho to approach them about a book contract. I've queried them about that for the last five years, at least, and never even received an answer back. Well, too bad for them. Now for sure, I'll try again.

Often American poets and writers bravely face the theme of mortality toward the close of their lives (Raymond Carver), on the battlefield (Wilfred Owen), or in dire illness (Jane Kenyon). But, like Emily Dickinson, BAM poets continuously looked at death, farewell, and departure, and created a poetry of disengagement from a toxic and disparaging culture. In her life and her work, my friend faced adversity with hopeful knowing.

> Feb 25, 2010
> Finally I'm back to life again, back to reality as the song says. Last night I read poetry with Sonia Sanchez and Angela Jackson and the day before I was so sick and had been so sick for weeks, I could hardly do nothing. They put some happy gas in my IV, gave me 2 pints/units of blood and I was good to go. I think I'm just coming down. Only to hear from Sonia at the poetry reading that Lucille Clifton made her commitment/ or transition as some people call it.
>
> Girl Things are happening. I know everybody was watching me these last few weeks and quiet as it's kept, I been watching some of them. I am trying to enjoy life as much as I can. I'm taking it easy. I'm laughing, and I think this is the way. I have to watch my blood pressure now. My feet are so swollen I cannot even get them in my boots. My legs are swollen too. I have to take diuretics and then run run run to guess where. I just laugh it off. What else is new?

We kept in contact until a few weeks before she died on April 2, 2010, in Chicago. She knew the seriousness of her illness and talked from her poet's soul of mortality. Throughout her final illness, she asked me to chant for her, promising she'd pray while I chanted.

> Feb 26, 2010
> Each day I am more impressed about youth and age. I am so glad I have been allowed to grow "old" shall we say? I love being an elder and I love the children. They are precious and I see me and others I know and don't know going and com-ing. You know what I mean? Somedays I want to say, this one or that one is back on earth again???? Let's hang in there. I feel so good today if only in my spirit and soul, well not only

but mostly. I fully plan to make it back to Oakland one day soon. It is one of my goals for 2010 or 2011, hopefully the former! I was telling Sonia S. I would love to host a gathering of Black women writers from the 60's and maybe not only Black... What do you think? I'm seriously sizing places trying to figure out how to pull it off. If you have any ideas about it, cue me in. Keep the faith.

Without the black women poets of the sixties breaking through, there would be no Beyoncé on the cover of TIME in her booty pants, no Audra MacDonald being the most celebrated Broadway actress ever, no Mae Jemison astronaut falling gracefully in space, no Oprah and Gayle/paradigmatic girlfriends influencing cultural politics, no Sistah Souljah being called out by a faux-black Bill Clinton, no Salt-N-Pepa, Cheryl James Sandra Denton and Deidra Roper ("Salt," "Pepa," and "DJ Spinderella") talking provocatively and gyrating their pelvises exponentially harder than Elvis. Black women strippers, derisively called "shake dancers," and blues singers had gotten down and dirty behind closed doors in the repressive decades before the sixties. But Salt-N-Pepa weren't marginalized and hidden from public view. They engaged sexually, though not politically. Rodgers, Sanchez, Wanda Coleman, Jayne Cortez, Shange, June Jordan et al, opened the political door, and like other affirmative action babies, Salt-N-Pepa walked through with nonchalance, becoming the first female rap group with huge hits in the US and United Kingdom.

> Ah, push it, ah, push it
> Ooh, baby, baby, baby, baby
> Ooh, baby, baby, baby, baby
> Get up on this.
> Ah, push it, ah, push it
> Ah, push it
>
> —Salt-N-Pepa

Whatever happened to Carolyn M. Rodgers?
She transcended herself.

And like many, she was overjoyed at Barack Obama's Presidential election.

Nov 10, 2008

How lucky I am! I was standing on the corner (Friday) where I live, which is directly across the street from where Obama goes to work out, when I look up and what do I see but a string of about 20 black, long limos, with Obama and God knows how many secret service men, and University of Chicago students of every race, creed, and color running along the street, wildly, holding up their cell phones with the cameras, yelling "I got one." I just there frozen in time, finally able to lift my arm and wave at this wonderful man in this long stream of sleek shiny black cars, policemen, in front and behind. I wish I had grandchildren to tell it to! It made my day you know and everybody else's, waiting for the bus!

Obviously, I live in a very posh neighborhood. Usually, I don't think much about it, because it is University turf and it's my SISTER's money, obviously not mine! Smile.
His neighborhood office is in the building on the sixteenth floor, and we look over at it from our living room. I calm myself, or I am constantly hyperventilating! Smile. What a world. What a life. Can't help lovin' it.

THE GUN AS ULTIMATE PERFORMANCE POEM

George Zimmerman killed Trayvon Martin, was acquitted for it, and has switched from security guard to painter, boxer, butcher, baker, candlestick-maker, whatever he wants. One round point blank to the chest = a perfect exchange. A young life for his art. The Gun as art and culture.

The Gun as work of art. The Gun as art form and genre. The Gun makes history. The Gun as steel metaphor carrying the human urge to dominate and lay waste to an enemy or perceived threat. Guns as import and export. Hollywood's Gun, its cinematic ordnance, is the United States' international calling card.

The Gun is oh-so-social, as it erases human inequality. Anyone can obtain one and point…shoot…kill. A bullet has no name, face, race, gender or class. The Gun is its microphone, the shooter but the stand for the microphone. The bullet is absolute, life-ending or life-changing, irreversible. The Gun is clean, leaving only smoke and powder in its wake. The Gun is the ultimate performance poem; the message in the poem is the bullet.

As much as I think I'm peaceable, I keep falling in with The Gun.

I moved back to my parents' house in East Oakland in 1990, in the middle of an intense drug war. My childhood home was a stone's throw from the notorious projects where heroin kingpin Felix Mitchell, as head of the 69 Mob, created an industry of drug trafficking as efficient for a decade as Henry Ford's assembly line. Felix the Cat's death in 1986 had left a fierce turf war in its wake. The nightly sequence I heard from my writing desk was spine-chilling: rapid machine gun fire, a car burning rubber as it screeched into the dark, silence for 10-12 minutes, then the ambulance siren. I never heard screams. Why were there no screams?

Without the noble purpose I conceived them to have when I was a young black militant, without art or revolutionary credo, these guns were unbearable microphones for a shattering community. Guns. Guns. Guns. I had liked guns.

Decades earlier, while a college junior, I joined the Black Panther Party in 1967 right when it split from a rival group of black cultural nationalists. Malcolm X's widow, Betty Shabazz, had come to San Francisco that February for a celebration of his life. One group called itself the Black Panther Party of Northern California, the other the Black Panther Party for Self-Defense; each agreed to meet her plane at the San Francisco airport with guns to protect her. One group showed up with loaded guns, the second came unloaded. The second group had no art, no ability to make history, no message. Though the second group was full of poets, writers, intellectuals and bright young minds, the first group prevailed and Huey Newton, Bobby Seale and Eldridge Cleaver joined the pantheon of holders of The Gun. The activists upstaged the artists/intellectuals. I had immense sympathy for the second group but pitied them (Pitied their women more. How much subservience would soothe a wounded ego?). The Gun was the shatterer of the boundary between the personal and the political. I liked guns. They were talismanic and palm-friendly. I liked being clandestine, carrying that .22 in my clutch purse when I went to work at the post office. The BPP labeled the intellectuals "paper panthers." This conflict between conscience and activism is not new. Stephen Spender, writing about the Oxford intellectuals said "detached intelligence" was a stance that a generation of anti-Fascists in the 1920s and 1930s rejected: "...personal values had to be sacrificed to the public cause. All that mattered was to defeat Fascism....choices had to be decided by the Marxist interpretation of history. Subjective motives did not count."

The split between the two groups of black militants shattered the viability of "detached intelligence" in the San Francisco Bay Area. The BPP cut through the pacifistic and rhetorical gestures and stance of the cultural nationalists with the pragmatism of the bullet. It resolved the issue of activism. How active should an activist be? Ready to die for the cause. The BPP resurrected the spirit of Nat Turner, Sojourner Truth and Harriet Tubman. The latter told her charges who wanted to return to the plantation once they'd gone underground: If you turn back, I'll shoot you.

The idea of carrying a loaded gun in May, 1967, into the legislative chambers of Sacramento, the dominion of Gov. Ronald Reagan, into the harsh deadly face of mid-20th century racist stolidity, rocked the world. Thirty black men, armed to the teeth and dressed in the signature beret and leather jackets, had the kind of impact that suicide bombers or serial killers have today. Scary.

The Gun is a revolt of the mind, an expulsion of hatred and thus a cleansing agent. Once it is fired, the act done, the two opposites are united forever, the killer and the killed written into history, memorialized or castigated.

To shun The Gun is to fear recklessness, to abhor chaos. Yet activists, oft called anarchistic, despise artists who don't overtly join them. Stanley Kunitz contends, "In a revolutionary period the activists are understandably disappointed in artists who do not overtly serve their movement. The Irish fighters for freedom despised [poet William Butler] Yeats for his failure to give them his unqualified support, not realizing that it was he who would immortalize their names and their cause…"

Bertolt Brecht said that a "conversation about trees is almost a crime because it involves keeping silent about so many misdeeds." The Black House in San Francisco flourished for a very short period (not as long as Felix Mitchell's drug empire) in 1966-67. I was there and no one was talking trees. Eldridge Cleaver's book *Soul on Ice* was a bestseller and playwright Marvin X had plays on at SF State and in community theaters. They formed The Black House and opened it up for readings, political education classes, poetry and dance performances, jazz and lectures. In the Fillmore District, the Black House was a seemingly perfect black counterpart for the hippie and drug-oriented Haight-Asbury. But its split was not only political; in retrospect, its air had a chauvinist aura. Women were often ornamental, breeders not warriors, cooks and clericals, servers not speakers, as if there to divert the heavy thinkers from the heavy biz of the day—fighting the man.

Many cultural nationalists—LeRoi Jones [Amiri Baraka], Don Lee [Haki Madhubuti], Sonia Sanchez—were poets, and poets were the shining lights of the Black Arts Movement. Kunitz points out that the writer works alone, unlike other workers, and the poet is even more exceptional: "Among writers the poet is freer than his brothers the novelist and playwright, because his work, unlike theirs, is practically worthless as a commodity. He is less subject than they to the pressure to modify the quality of his work in order to produce an entertainment. Nothing he can do will make his labor profitable. He might as well yield to the beautiful temptation to strive towards the purity of an absolute art."

Thus we see the Black Arts Movement and its relation to the BPP, the poets and dramatists stand in stark counterpoint. As student activists at SF State, the Black Student Union fought to bring Jones, Lee and Sanchez onto campus. We formed the Black Arts and Culture Troupe and toured community centers throughout the Bay Area with poetry, dance, and agit prop plays. We enacted ideas we were hearing on soapboxes about black power, black consciousness, and black beauty. We staged the conflagrations that were taking place in urban cities. We were empowering ourselves, our communities and getting academic credit. A natural progression was community activism. In 1967, my roommates and I joined the Black Panther Party which we found far more than a linguistic call to arms. It was a family, the place where you get together on holidays, tolerate the bigmouths, take care of each other, and keep it in the family, i.e. the secrets, the dirty laundry, the drunks, the incest, the beatings. Robyn

Spencer, who interviewed former Black Panther women in the 1990s for her doctoral research, commented at our final interview that she was frustrated by our overall lack of forthrightness. I reminded her that there is no statute of limitations on murder, not that I knew of any such event.

However, the most important idea from that time, as I told another interviewer, was that we changed the language, the way black people thought and spoke, the way black people thought about how they were spoken about. A major assault on oppression is to assault it linguistically. Pre-Edward Said's *Orientalism*, two black males from the flatlands of Oakland, California, gave a voice to the oppressed using English in a wholly new way. Jean-Paul Sartre said the oppressed gain the use of the oppressor's language. In one instant, *Off the Pig* tossed back all the awful, dehumanizing, negative ways African-Americans had been characterized for two centuries. Baboons, coons, animals. To come up with this one phrase to describe abominable *behavior*, not physicality, was genius.

In *Virgin Soul*, my coming-of-age novel about that time, I handle The Gun often. The narrative would have lost its essence if I hadn't. At one point, protagonist Geniece shows her proper aunt the very first Black Panther Party newspaper. Her aunt recoils at the blood, guts and violence in Emory Douglas' artwork, with its copious use of the steely black metaphor. The Gun was an actual weapon carried and maintained by party members. It was Art. It was Metaphor. It was loaded with meaning and death.

The use of language and ritual had awed me in childhood where I loved communal gatherings, gospel fests, familial and religious celebrations. I'd worked since high school as a journalist butbecame disgusted with the narrow scope of the field, its all-whiteness, sameness and predictability. Assigned to edit the BPP newspaper, I found myself embedded in the inner workings of the party, typing, retyping, printing words and phrases like *off the pigs. Power to the people. All power to the people. Free Huey.*

My hands shocked me as they lettered and typed these words and the manifestos they formed. The BPP was appropriating the oppressor's language and using it to shatter oppression. This new use of language by the BPP was as powerful as The Gun and even more so because it aroused feeling and changed the terms of discourse between friends, enemies, lovers, generations and cultures. Being an agent of change meant I aroused deep feeling, affected discourse, found the powerful voices that I had heard in childhood, in church, in soul music, in the pulpit - within my own voice. Thus empowered, I began writing poetry, essays, and eventually moved on to drama and fiction, my start as a writer.

Some would whitewash the civil rights movement and Dr. Martin Luther King Jr. into benign icons of a distant era, outsized statues or memories for annual celebration. Some would not see the movements for civil rights and black power nor the varied tactics of the NAACP, SCLC, SNCC, BPP, CORE, the Urban League, and the Nation of Islam as a spectrum of resistance against the racism that determined every facet of American life. The Black Panther Party for Self-Defense was the fist (The Gun, loaded, that is) of the kid (black people) who has been bullied (racism, oppression, legalized discrimination) long enough by the outsized bully on the block (US govt., US Constitution until 1865, opponents of Radical Reconstruction, Jim Crow, KKK, Bull Connor, etc.). Power concedes nothing with a demand, Frederick Douglass said. To demand is not to ask or beseech. That time when the streets were packed with citizens, students, protestors, workers, mothers against the war, unionists was not an acquiescent moment in this country's history. The numerous deaths are memorialized and well-documented. Did the moment peter out? Vanish into thin air? Not quite. The principles spread into society.

From the virgin soil of turbulence came the second wave of feminism and gay rights movements. The disabled emerged from seclusion and institutions to lobby for public access and accommodations. Senior citizens became Gray Panthers. Maria Gillan [a friend and fellow poet] became Maria Mazziotti Gillan, reclaiming her Italian-American roots and triggering the ethnic white literary movement at once. Bilingualism and Ebonics became recognized as essential curricula. *Caucus* as an intransitive verb meant your group agenda had to be strengthened privately and exhaustively to have maximum impact. *Self*-help, *self*-empowerment and *self*-enhancement became ideals because an entire society had watched the 97-pound weakling (black people) go from chump to champ. Black music, musicians and dancers became ambassadors-at-large to American society and the world. Duke Ellington and Count Basie had been there, done that. But the airwaves and new media amplified the beat, the dances, the Soul Train lines, the frizzy hair, the handshakes, the lingo (*bro*), none of which needed The Gun or its bullet because the BPP had handled that task. Our current heated debate about the n-word is permissible because of the BPP and Black Arts and Culture movement. Ishmael Reed, in grand old man fashion, came out with *Writing is Fighting: Thirty-Seven Years of Boxing on Paper* in 1988. The feat of aging gives one that Yeatsian right to write the story.

A few years ago, I woke up surrounded by Guns. Guns. Guns. My boss at the state arts council hosted me at her South Jersey home during my artist-in-residency. We'd had a falling out after her son had been killed in a hunting accident and she'd had three months of disarray and grief. Without money to meet my basic expenses and no checks coming in, my capacity for sympathy plunged. Angry words ensued. Eventually we made up. She invited me to her beautiful, starkly contemporary home nestled in the woods. We drank wine and talked late into the night; I looked through photo albums as she recounted how her grown children had been hunting when one fired the bullet that ricocheted and hit her son. He died in surgery. I went to sleep in the spare bedroom, too tired to take a good look around me. I woke up an hour later and turned on the light. The room was decorated with guns—handguns, rifles and guns with bayonets mounted in wooden and glass cases. I was sleeping in an ordnance. I tried to fall asleep but couldn't dispel the images. In the moonlight I saw that the sheets on my bed had gun insignias all over them. For a moment, I thought I had gone crazy. Gun sheets? I had to do some serious calming down. The guns on the sheets and the walls were art, fashion and memorabilia.

I liked guns. I like mystery, intrigue, even devilment. My father was an avid reader of westerns, thrillers and detective novels. He had stacks of them next to his side of the bed. My mother had Bibles, loads of them, modern ones, illustrated ones, King James Version. As far as I could tell he never read from her side, and she never read any of his books…complete opposites married for 50 years. There was no gun. My mother said we couldn't even have sharp knives because tempers were too short in our household.

I would like a society without The Gun. Too many short tempers in the world and this society. The BPP had a message that was received. As it deepened its focus in community service, the guns became purely metaphoric and the party split into factions for and against The Gun. Internecine rivalries sprung up. I had moved far away spatially and spiritually.

I don't want gun control. I want police who are unarmed, peace officers. We can't have that unless we do away with guns. Maybe we can have parks where people play with guns the way we play with dinosaurs. That sounds like a shooting range. But it wouldn't be for target practice. It would be for fun. It wouldn't be a rehearsal for cruelty.

When Trayvon Martin was killed by The Gun, my heart ached. Trayvon was at risk because he didn't know how to cower, a posture that my generation destroyed. He didn't turn tail and run – although he might just have been shot in the back; he didn't *yessuh* back stepping. He fought George Zimmerman, toe-to-toe, and Zimmerman fired The Gun, at point blank range, because that was his creative moment. His high art. His historical moment. George Zimmerman united with his opposite Trayvon Martin forever. And the performances continue, in Aurora, Illinois, in Newtown, Connecticut, in schools and theaters and public spaces throughout the country. I liked guns. I hate The Gun.

ECONOMIC GUERILLA WARFARE:
What it is and why we need it

As soon as school starts and Labor Day slips by, Christmas begins. Stores, merchants, corporations, the American economy are geared to get everyone – regardless of gender, race, age, income – into a mindless frenzy of shopping. It starts with the build-up to Halloween, Thanksgiving, Christmas and New Year's, a treadmill of debt, guilt, drinking, sugar overload, all helped by advertising to numb our minds and dumb down our common sense.

In December, 2014, after yet another disgusting round of cop killings, I joined a protest for Eric Garner against Macy's because it was the big box store in Times Square. I cut up my Macy's card so I wouldn't be tempted. Being a dyed-in-the-wool Macy's shopper, pulling into the mall and ducking into Macy's in San Leandro, Hayward or Walnut Creek has been one of my secret pleasures, immensely gratifying, stress-relieving retail therapy. To delay that gratification was extremely meaningful. And it hurt.

GRAPES, LETTUCE AND MACY'S

I boycotted grapes for the five years it took for Cesar Chavez, the United Farm Workers union and concerned Californians to shake our fist in the face of the grape and lettuce growers. And I love grapes, have a pound in my crisper right now. I joined the month-long boycott of Target after Philando Castile and Alton Erving were killed by police in Minneapolis and Baton Rouge. I just couldn't take one more bullet from a cop's gun going pointblank into a black body. Someone called me irrational and kneejerk for doing this and suggested I boycott Apple instead, then said coolly that she didn't "believe in boycotts anyway"!

Another asked what Macy's had to do with Michael Brown's killing. Good question. I want to hit em where it hurts. I'm not for violence, don't want to go to jail, I'll be frank. I like creature comforts, lah de dah. However, this country runs on moolah. If money is disturbed, people pay attention. For the Christmas that starts Sept. 8 and ends on New Year's Day, if enough of us boycott big box stores, retailers will beg for relief - from their local grand juries, police departments, city councils, and politicians everywhere. We can't just wring our hands and reflect on man's inhumanity to man. We know it all too well now. Yes, black-on-black crime is horrid also, but this legalized killing can't be tolerated any longer.

Heroin was no big deal when it was contained to the Harlems of the world and jazz musicians. Then "white kids" found drugs in the sixties – a Diane Linkletter jumping to her death on LSD - and their parents, alerted to the peril, pushed for prevention, clinics, all manner of remedy. I'd hate to think that cop killings have to escalate with white males, 15-19, or some such demographic, before the slumbering beast of public opinion awakens to the hard fact that the police have way too much power - for anyone's good.

To be honest, boycotting big box stores is a piece with my radical history, childhood hardships, and innate frugality. We Americans here in the USA don't realize how much world citizens in disadvantaged nations sacrifice and suffer for our bounty, our aisles and aisles of packaged foods, coffee, scotch tape, electronics and appliances, candles, bath products, liquor, furniture, toys, cars, etc., etc. Think Ikea. Think Costco. Think Macy's.

A DIFFERENT KIND OF PRAYER
At our holiday meals, just one person who understands this disparity needs to say that before or after prayer (or in place of):

youth, children and poor people the world over are slaving right now so we can "enjoy" the holidays. What bittersweet freedom we have. We need to check ourselves every time we sit down to feast, every time we open the mailbox and get a circular from J.C. Penney or L.L.Bean. I love material comfort as much as anyone. I'm doing this on my IPad chillaxing on my SertaPerfectSleeper underneath my lovely quilts, handmade in India, from Macy's bedding dept. But I hate it when we don't acknowledge in thought, word and deed that our fortune too often comes from someone else's misfortune.

And another damn thing. This IS GENOCIDE. "Police officers, security guards, or self-appointed vigilantes extrajudicially killed at least 313 African-Americans in 2012," according to a recent study. This means a black person was killed by a security officer every 28 hours. http://www.occupy.com/article/black-man-killed-us-every-28-hours-police#sthash.VWYsDVid.dpuf

The Federal Bureau of Investigation's Supplementary Homicide Report found "1,217 deadly police shootings from 2010 to 2012 captured in the federal data show that blacks, age 15 to 19, were killed at a rate of 31.17 per million, while just 1.47 per million white males in that age range died at the hands of police."
www.propublica.org/article/deadly-force-in-black-and-white

Darren Wilson, the Ferguson police officer who killed Michael Brown, testified that Brown was like a demon charging at him. Hitler and the Nazis reduced the Jews to animals, rats specifically, the easier to justify exterminating them. Very ominous.

A DESENSITIZING PROCESS

And this fad of enlarging buttocks/lips/breasts to stupendous proportions is connected to the gunning down of blacks. Our natural traits are seen as grotesque, as grotesqueries, as "things" to be sensationalized and put on display, ridiculed, sold, exploited, Hottentotted...dehumanized. When we're not seen regularly as human beings who feel pain, sorrow, joy, beauty, we're killed the same way animals and insects are killed by human beings, i.e. when man needs to eat them, tires of them, fears them, cannot afford them anymore or is irritated by them.

No one is going to kill Kim Kardashian because she had her butt blown up and parades it around. But her act of mocking the black derriere makes a lasting impact that says a black woman's ass is a commodity to be sold to the highest bidder and is a sexual fetish. Not a black woman's whole body even, just the ass, baby, the height of being objectified. Kim can deflate her rear whenever she chooses and go back to flatville while we've been cut into pieces by this object-commodification.

An entire category of people is being reduced to caricature. The more vulnerable we are, the easier to target. And it won't always be the black guys in white tees, dreads and sagging pants. Black children and elders are killed routinely by the police too. We're not far from the 1800s, slavery, the failed radical reconstruction, the hatred of poor whites toward the *middle-class blacks* for their economic progress. Remember, they lynched black storeowners and artisans. We can't forget that black Wall Street, America's wealthiest black community, was terrorized and burned down by angry white mobs, May 31—June 1, 1921, in Greenwood, Oklahoma.

We are supposed to be a nation of laws. But when those laws are administered unfairly, we have the democratic duty to protest. It's about the police not being judge-jury-executioner. Michael Brown in Ferguson, Alton Sterling in Baton Rouge, Philando Castile in Minneapolis could've been wrong, but it's not up to the cops to administer justice. My beautiful grandson and my wonderful son could be on the ground, dead, for four hours, shot down, because some cop overstepped his bounds. This isn't about one person, though for their parents it is. This principle of injustice being meted out by people whose salaries are paid by public taxes, of justice being rigged by the prosecutor who was supposed to be objective in the grand jury proceedings, has to be exposed and understood.

We can't just tell all black people: go back to abject humility, silence in the face of brutality, keep your head down at all times. Yes, indeed, Black people used to be the model minority. We worked hard, kept our nose to the grindstone, suffered in silence, had strong community unity, albeit forced by segregation (like the Chinatowns, Japantowns, Koreatowns which, after two or three generations, lose ground because the second and third generations assimilate and move away). We patronized black businesses; we stayed in our place all the way to the segregated cemeteries. It's all changed. We can't go back. We ain't going back. We have to keep it moving. After all, those are our sons and daughters being strangled to death for selling loose ciggies, shot nine times in the back because...just because. No reason, but a definite rhyme. This is about color in America. This is about dark skin. This is about the stigmata of brown skin. It's not erasable. When we walk in a store, theater, park, our history walks in with us, alongside us, in front of us. It introduces us. Not our peacefulness or our politeness or our profession. We are at war. Not with people, with the mind of ignorance, hate, indifference, callousness, cruelty. Those of us who see this cancer, these cancers, growing have to take action. We can't reverse history. We are free but we have to fight with all our might to protect that hard won freedom.

ORANGE JUICE AND FLORIDA JUSTICE

Let's not forget we the people exerted our power in Florida in bringing George Zimmerman before the courts. I started a meme-NO JUSTICE NO JUICE to boycott Florida orange juice until Zimmerman was brought to justice in Florida. It came back my way a week later in a beautiful graphic meme that spread like wildfire. How can we hit them where it hurts? I'm for nonviolent tactics, and I know money talks.

Michael Brown. Oscar Grant. Eric Garner. And the beat goes

on? I don't think so. The blatant disregard for justice by the St. Louis county failed grand jury cannot be ignored or we put our youth, ourselves, at continued risk.

A friend asked after Baton Rouge, Minneapolis and Dallas: Why won't they let us live and love and raise our children? Why?

I replied: Because, "they" in their arrogance think that we've become dispensable. That's what all the appropriation is about. If they could clone us, they would. But, dammit, we have incredible genetic and spiritual staying power. "They" have had the upper hand from ca.14th century but understand, in evolutionary and scientific ways, the tables are turning. E.g., imminent climate change could bring a new Ice Age to Northern Europe, forcing whole populations to migrate south to northern Africa...yes, a complete reversal of the current immigration pattern. Read deeper into why the elites wanted EU and the common people wanted Brexit. It was about consolidation of power. The old NATO agreement was for the US to police the world, and European countries to divert their military monies into social programs. That worked for 40 years until the 1% got greedy, saw the imbalance in population growth, and decided to set up this century the way the robber barons set up their holdings in the 19th century. We black Africans are simply the canary in the coal mine. They keep trying out tactics on us, from enslavement and breeding, to the Tuskegee Syphilis Study, measles vaccines, Henrietta Lacks, vesico-vaginal fistula experiments (sans anesthesia), Sara Baartman the 'Hottentot Venus' whose sexual organs and buttocks generated extensive science during and after her life, mass incarceration of Black men, heroin, crack cocaine flooding the black community, purposeful neglect of the flood barriers in NOLA's Ninth Ward, charter schools, police oppression, etc. After these last few killings, you ask, "How much more can we take?" Turn that into scientific hypothesis: how much torture can this subculture [blacks] endure before it crumbles or fights back? Though I find it hard to believe this is some master plan, I do believe that dominance and weakness are genetically determined.

I hear police helicopters circling my neighborhood about 8 minutes from downtown Oakland. At any time a city can be shut down like Boston was after the marathon bombings, like Philly after Mayor Gray bombed MOVE, like Tulsa in 1921 when the city of black millionaires was bombed.

We cannot drug ourselves with Xmas and wake up to find the New Year even worse. Cancer doesn't go away. The malignancy grows, even while the politicians and plutocrats manipulate the quadrennial freak show called the Presidential primaries.

Show the outrage Pray Protest Organize Empathize Teach our young our history Register to vote Champion literacy All power to the people Understand police oppression is systemic We need to attack it systemically We need to prevail upon all of our existing rights-organizations, committees, civic groups, elected reps, newspapers, blogs, co-workers, fellow students, peers and families Put the pressure on each police dept. & city council in a city where black youths live [HAH!] Show up at public meetings Boycott Vote Be agents for change wherever we are.

A SCRIPT FOR THE PRESS:
Answering Questions about *Virgin Soul*

My Viking Editor had me prepare a script for media interviews. It came in ultra handy.

- What was the inspiration behind *Virgin Soul*?

I joined the Black Panther Party when I was 20. And at 23, I became the youngest faculty member of the nation's first Black studies Department at San Francisco State. By the time I was 24, 25, I realized just how historic the time was and I began to write down important recollections.

- Have events from your life shaped the characters or events in *Virgin Soul*?

There was a place called The Black House in San Francisco in the Fillmore. I never forgot the first time I went. It was an immersion in black consciousness: speeches, dancers and drummers. The clothing, the radical posters, the African clothing, the large amber necklaces and sculptured earrings –all these images stayed with me.

- How much of *Virgin Soul* is based on personal experience?

Many events in the novel I experienced, saw or heard about.

At San Francisco State, there were rallies every day, TV and radio trucks at the school daily. My parents feared for my safety but they used to say they could see me on the 6 o'clock news.

    • *Virgin Soul* takes place during a historic period in America at the heart of the Black Power Movement. What kind of research did you do before you began writing?

Research: I used old Black Panther Party newspapers, Huey Newton's archives at Stanford University, the California History Room at the Oakland Public Library, and archives at Merritt College and at SFSU.

    • Very few novels have been written about female Black Panther members. Is Geniece's character loosely based on your own personal experiences?

    • How did you build Geniece's character?

She has my impudence and curiosity. But I deliberately made Geniece dark-skinned so I could address the issue of skin color, or colorism, in the black community.

And I made her more introspective than I was during that time.

    • Do you consider Geniece representative of women during this period?

Certain images have become iconic to the movement: Huey Newton in the peacock chair, the rows of men in black berets. But women were integral to the entire movement. Geniece is the voice of the story that hasn't been told about the Black Panthers.

    • How important was the setting?

Setting is everything in *Virgin Soul*. I first met Huey and Bobby at Oakland City College, now Merritt College. I'd see all these soapbox orators on the front lawn of the college. They were entertaining. My friends and I came out from our classes just to gawk. I didn't intend to become a radical, didn't know that Merritt College was, as The Attorney General of California said, a hotbed of radicalism. The seeds of the Black Panther Party were in Oakland and at Merritt College.

• Do you feel as though San Francisco became somewhat of its own character in the novel?

SF becomes the place where Geniece grows up. There she encounters the harshness of life vs. the ideals she encounters at the community college. SF and Haight Ashbury are distinct from the BPP movement.

• Are there any particular moments or experiences in *Virgin Soul* that were difficult emotionally to write?

Death scenes are difficult but fascinating. Getting the details just right.

• Which characters do you identify most with and why?

I loved Geniece's relatives. They're earthy and love cooking and having big dinners. They resemble my own family and other families I've known.

• Could you discuss your experience writing your first novel?

I write at night often. Sitting at my dining room table. First I outline, then jot down dialogue and bits and pieces of scenes on Post-Its, then gather it all together and write out a scene.

I listen to music from radio stations that play 60s and 70s music.

My playlist for this novel would include:

"California Dreamin'", "Don't Look Back" (The Temptations), "Somebody to Love" (Jefferson Airplane), "Mustang Sally" (Wilson Picket), "Do Right Woman, Do Right Man" (Aretha Franklin), "Bad Moon Rising" (Creedence Clearwater Revival), "People Get Ready" (The Impressions), "What a Wonderful World" (Louis Armstrong), "My Favorite Things" (John Coltrane), "I Was Made to Love Her" (Stevie Wonder), "It's Your Thing" (The Isley Brothers), "Cupid" (Sam Cooke), "Mrs. Robinson" (Simon & Garfunkel), "When Something is Wrong With My Baby" (Sam & Dave), "Hot Fun in the Summertime" (Sly and the Family Stone), "Linus & Lucy" (Vince Guaraldi Trio), "At Last" (Etta James) [and I love Phoebe Snow's version] and "A Change Is Gonna Come" (Sam Cooke).

- How did your writing process change compared to writing poems or plays?

Time is the great difference. I can write a poem in a matter of a day or two, even though I may go back and edit over a longer period. I have written a full length play in ten weeks. That works. For the novel, it took years to get it right.

ALL THE WOMEN IN MY FAMILY READ TERRY McMILLAN

I'm a black writer of literary fiction. My novel was published by Viking in 2013. I'm thrilled. But what a mission. The black chick lit phenomenon, heralded by Terry McMillan's *Waiting to Exhale* in 1992, exploded and led to new genres-urban fiction, street lit, gangsta fiction-which now overshadow African-American literary fiction. The new genres have box office clout. A black female writer not writing chick lit has an uphill challenge. The proliferation of largely female black book clubs ensures that these novels are instructing a significant part of the black reading community.

It's ironic that these new genres have come to represent the whole of contemporary black literature. Langston Hughes honored the black vernacular and constructed "an entire literary tradition upon the actual spoken language of the black working and rural classes—the same vernacular language that the growing and mobile black middle classes considered embarrassing and demeaning."[1] The confining currently popular genres use selective pieces of the "actual spoken language" of a class of black people, which accounts in part for their colorful appeal. But the works often treat complexity and individuality elliptically. Yet they're popular. When I went to visit a male relative in the county jail and asked how he was faring, he replied that he had found a book by Omar Tyree and, by the way, jail wasn't all bad. Yet even McMillan has expressed disapproval of her literary progeny:

> There are a lot of fine young new African-American
> writers out here. [But] I am not a fan of ghetto and urban
> lit.... I take seriously what they're writing about in terms

of inner city life and all that. But I don't like the way that they tell their stories. It's not very redeeming. It seems that they glorify violence and hatred and self-hatred to me, to be very honest. And sex is gratuitous. I don't like the exploitation of black women's bodies on the covers of all the books that they use to sell them. And to me a lot of them are poorly written and unedited. And I think as black people we've struggled too long and too hard to try to be decent people and treat each other with a lot more respect and dignity. And these books just fall so short of it. It's almost as if they [the authors] don't even believe that we deserve it. [2]

Black literature, which I first devoured in the 60s/70s, included African-American speech in the urban zones, Adrienne Kennedy writing "The Funnyhouse of the Negro," the beat poetry of Bob Kaufman, the black nationalist ravings of Amiri Baraka, Ba'hai-influenced poetry of Robert Hayden, the chants of Sterling Brown, Gwendolyn Brooks' window on Chicago in poetry, and yes, Iceberg Slim's pimps. We were universal. There was no disconnecting Aimé Cesaire and Wole Soyinka's work and Claude Brown's *Manchild in the Promised Land*. We were part of a diaspora. We're still part of that; the whole of our literature isn't a trend.

In an ongoing attempt to counteract the trend, I have used my own writing and my teaching to reach this very population that the publishing industry has targeted. Being a community college English instructor for nineteen years, I encounter a young to middle-aged demographic that is urban, literate, and decidedly not highbrow. I see my students carrying and reading what some call "thug fiction." My Oakland, California, school, an open campus in the heart of the city, has roughly a third African-American, a third Asian American, and a third "other"-that includes whites and Native Americans. I cannot nor do I want to avoid their lives in literature.

I regularly use texts that I hope will broaden their perspective (what teacher doesn't do that?). *Rosa Lee: a mother and her family in urban America* by Leon Dash and *Makes Me Wanna Holler* by Nathan McCall are as gritty, provocative, urban and in-your-face as any street fiction, yet they are greater teaching tools. James MacBride's *Color of Water* and Frank McCourt's *Angela's Ashes* strip poverty to its naked truth but their stronger literary elements illuminate the human condition.

Recently I ended my summer classes by having the students in my freshman English composition class produce two of my own short plays at the college. They were leaping over each other to fulfill the demands of theatre. I rarely see such joy in students. One brought in medical uniforms for the hospital play from her vocational college where she was responsible for uniforms. Drama allowed them to push beyond their limits and exult in the abstract needs of the plays. It brought me joy too.

These then are my concerns. I don't want my tribe[s] to be squashed into a tiny space. That's been our history. We don't have to do it to ourselves. The detailing of the complexity and richness in human nature seems to be the regular province of literature, more so than film or television. I strive to make that kind of contribution with my writing and my teaching.

[1] Henry Louis Gates Jr., <u>Langston Hughes, Critical Perspectives Past and Present</u>

[2]<u>http://link.brightcove.com/services/player/bcpid57408845001?bctid=613867137001</u>

FROM PORT ARTHUR, TEXAS TO OAKLAND: AN INTERVIEW WITH MY MOTHER-IN-LAW

"Half the people in California ain't got sense to pour piss out of a boot" —Charlene Thomas, age 93

P ort Arthur, Texas, was a company town where people worked for the oil companies, got up early, and went to bed early. It's a seaport town, surrounded by water, an abundance of seafood. Charlene Thomas, an Oakland resident from Port Arthur, said, every meal had

> *Some kind of water-something on your plate. Fish, shrimp, sausage and shrimp, all kind of goulashes, all done for 12 o'clock in the day which was the biggest meal.*

There they ate breakfast, dinner, and supper which was the lightest meal in early evening. Charlene, now 93 years old, came here in '42 at 13 years old, on, her first trip out of Texas to the train station at 16th and Wood in West Oakland. Daughter of a longshoreman, widow of a longshoreman, mother of a longshoreman, mother of five, grandmother of eight, and great grandmother to many beloveds, she moved to Oakland--with her mother, stepdad, and sisters-- in chain migration, in 1942. They were one family of many.

> *There were a lot of people trying to better themselves, especially black people, jumping in cars coming to California. A lot of them made it here, made their money and went on back home."* She stayed. *Of her adopted state, she says with a chuckle: "Half the people in California ain't got sense to pour piss out of a boot.*

Home was Port Arthur, a town near Beaumont, a seaport, and center of a large oil refinery network, including Gulf Oil. Charlene Thomas recalls the neighborliness, and that everybody was the same, neighborly, went to the beach together, celebrated Juneteenth, and socialized at church

What she missed most was walking and going wherever they wanted to go without having to get on a streetcar or the bus. It took her a long time, six or seven months, to get accustomed here. She tried to go home and go back to her dad in Port Arthur who told her, if you want to come home, you can. But it's better for you to stay with your mom. Because he worked all the time.

In Port Arthur you didn't have to get up and go anywhere. You just got on the phone and called, and everything was delivered, like Door Dash and Instacart now.

Only then, it was young kids making extra money delivering on bicycles, on little carts, bringing food, medicine. Some would deliver on foot.

In Oakland, though, you had to get up and go to the store.

Big stores like Swan's and Housewives Market. It wasn't all shopping. That's where everybody knew everybody and they'd sit and wait to see who had just come to town. Same with the train station, somebody new arriving just as she had from Port Arthur, on the Southern Pacific: Southerners, mostly old men, Charlene said, used to go to the rail station and just wait to see who came in on the train. Afterwards, the men would come by the house talking about who got off the train. Her own first impression getting off the train was:

Terrible. When we got here, I saw all these big old Victorian houses. No paint on them—they looked raggedy, and the train station on 16th & Wood didn't look nice. I was in jr. high, and thought, this is California, this ragged little town. Oh well, you gotta go where your parents go.

CHAIN MIGRATION

Her grandmother had come to Oakland to visit her sick daughter and decided to stay. At one point, it seemed to young Charlene that everybody wanted to move to California. Many were merchant seamen. After her grandmother came, she started pulling her children one by one. Charlene's mother was the last to come. Her stepdad worked on the port there and found he could transfer here. When he got here, he worked in the shipyards for about six months and then went to the port. He got his papers together in Port Arthur, where he belonged to the ILA, International Longshoremen's Association, and joined ILWU.

Port Arthur Was a Mixed Town

Her family always lived in the mixed area until the moved to the southern side where all the black folks lived. In Port Arthur, she recalls, they didn't have streetcars, just buses. But if you wanted to get to town or go anywhere, you didn't have to ride buses. The buses were segregated. Most of the black folks rode cabs. Or they walked. But they had more cab drivers in Port Arthur. The cabs had black drivers. Black folks were entrepreneurs; pharmacists had their own grocery stores, drugstores:

> *Across the track, that's where black folks had their own everything, funeral homes, hospitals. They had a clinic, what I call a hospital. If you got sick, you got a bed set up. But if you were deathly sick then you went to the bigger hospital.*

Charlene's grandmother, Mama Lucy, used to sell food, fried fish and chicken. And not from a fish market. People would bring her fish from the gulf. She'd pay them, cook it up, and then sell to the people who worked in the oil derricks. A truck would bring the oil workers for dinner at noon. But Mama Lucy was up before dawn. She'd set up that food table in the yard: vegetables, meat, cornbread, the fish, make a big bucket of tea, they'd come eat and the truck would take them back to the field. That's how her grandma made her living. Charlene said folks always could make some money.

> *My grandmother worked hard, I saw how she had to get up*

before day, lighting that stove, going out there getting that food, coming home cooking, ready by the time the people got there. I didn't want to cook for nobody but myself. Been around too many people cooking for somebody else, I just wanted to cook for my family.

Her grandmother lived a ways from them. Everybody had to get in a car to go wherever they went. Charlene said, every little town in Texas the same. One movie house-- white folks downstairs and colored upstairs, signs for Colored faucets. As a youngster she thought,

What's the difference in water? You got colored people all up in your house cooking and feeding you—y'all is some dumb ass white people.

BIG DIFFERENCES IN FOOD

In Port Arthur, they called gumbo cheap eating. And basically, the family cooks made their own gumbo; they could make a pot of gumbo in a minute cuz they were right at sea port land, not that high.

Now California was what I call mild-eating people, not highly seasoned food, no chili peppers and all that.

They could go out fishing—catch their own meal in an hour—come back home and be ready to cook it. That's what they used to do. Charlene recalls two little old ladies who used to go fishing early in the morning, crabbing and fishing with one of their granddaughters and herself. She was seven years old.

They'd say, I'm going crabbing in the morning. I'm a call ya. You did crabbing early, 6 am. By 7, you were heading home. It didn't take long. We would get up and go with them. Cause if you fishing you gonna hook some crabs…all you need is a net to catch them. Where we lived you just walk to go catch crab… crabbing was easy. Just take a string, go behind the grocery store, get a piece of meat throwed away, wrap it up, get you some twine, tie that meat on that twine, throw it in the water on the end of the pole…when you pull the net up you pull it up full of crabs. You couldn't go in the big channels where the big

ships would run the crabs away; you had to cross over the big
pathway, past the big ships, to get to the little ships.

But it was dangerous. They'd sit down on the steps on the seawall. Even though, the old folks told them not to go further, because if the ship came in, the water would rise, kids sat down and got wet. Sometimes they sat too close; they'd fall in; she never did. But there were always kids drowning, kids who didn't obey, very rarely old folk who knew better. She had her own bucket to bring home crabs live and crawling...dozens of little blue crabs...a bucket of little soft shelled blue crabs. She said;

When I came here and saw crabs here, I had never seen a crab
that big. They didn't have blue crabs when we came here, only
the big red ones.

Big Differences in Weather

There were huge differences in weather. Lightning and thunder in summer and winter-- in the South when it goes to lightening and thundering, you close up everything. It was very scary. They'd close the mirrors up; the dressers were made with the mirrors closed because the mirrors could draw the lightening. So they'd close the windows, pull the shades, go somewhere in the house and sit down and be quiet. Lightening would still come through, the sun would be shining. Then all of a sudden everything'd get dark. Charlene says:

You never get used to that. Here I think your body adjusts. I
used to always be cold here. But your body adjusts. I didn't like
humid, when it's hot and no sunshine, it's sticky heat, I hated it.
I call it wet summer.

As strong as the weather, and the differences in food, were her views on black people and white people.

Black folks are something, we can have our own country and
own town cuz they got more brains than the white man. I
learned that long time ago--white folk is dumb. Why they out
here just arguing and picking at people? They mad cuz you
got a better looking house. I don't care what you did to black
people, their house look better than them trashy white people.

I'm just talking about the South, where we lived. They always lived on the main street but you lived in the alley. But we lived better than them. They might be living on the front street, but they was trifling and not fixing they self up. But the average one that's like that, they all hang together in their own little nasty neighborhood. You can always tell where they live because they nasty, they junky, they don't clean up, but where black folks lived was always nice. I don't care if it was a two roomer, yard cleaned up, even if they didn't have grass, swept. Black folks are proud people. Their house ain't gonna be junkied up, not in that little town where I came from.

Biggest Difference: People's Friendliness

The biggest difference was in people's friendliness in California. She didn't find people in California very friendly. She said,

You could always tell people that weren't from California, they were open and friendly. California people were kind of selfish, clannish, stick to themselves. They don't mingle with nobody else. They think they're better than anybody else. And half of em ain't got sense enough to pour piss out of a boot. You talk about people out of the South, you need to take a trip to the South and learn something. You been here all your life and you don't own a home. You go to the South and everybody in the South owns a home.

The worst thing about California was that the more black people came here, the more prejudice there was. California got prejudiced. When her family first got here, it wasn't that bad. Then it got to the place, where, like if you went in the store, they'd take their time to wait on you.

I just felt like they were thinking it's too many black people. When the white folk moved out [in the 60s] and black folks went to buying these houses, it was a lot of white folks still here. But after a while they got to moving like flies, I didn't care, I didn't care nothing about them living near me no way.

But would she move back? That's the question.

Nobody went back down there. Wasn't nothing to go back down there for, wasn't nothing in those little towns.

The Greatest Thing about California: the Parks

By far, the greatest thing about California and what brings a pure smile to her face—the weather and the parks. When her husband got off work, they'd pack up food and go,

I love these parks, they were so big. We lived in the parks in Oakland, up and down the coasts, in the valley. I raised my kids in parks. We ate more meals in the park than anything; my kids loved to feed the ducks at Lake Merritt. Every park you could go to, I've been in them. I'd light a fire and grill, then we'd get home and I'd give the kids a bath. We used to get up on Saturdays, pack a lunch and go to the parks. Every time we passed a park, we'd say we can come back to this park. I'd come out with a book while the children played. People say everything costs so much money but parks are free.

In the long run, do you have a better life because of the move?

Yes, I'm sure. Not really materially so much. Just being peaceful and satisfied.

LETTER TO A NEWLY-MINTED PH.D.: WE WON
(Dr. Kim McMillon asked me if we won the revolution)

Dec 12, 2024

Dear Kim,

I thought of your question about whether we won the revolution as I read an article in *The NY Times* about a successful young black couple. **We won, yes we did.** These two bright young people are the testament to that: young millennials look at them. We won the cultural revolution: she is dark skinned and beautiful, something not celebrated in the decades before the 60s. We won in academia (you yourself, Dr. McMillon, picking up your doctorate at UC Merced, are testament to that); he is a lawyer from Brooklyn, a rarity and near impossibility before we busted down the doors with open enrollment. They are living together, not married. That's the sexual revolution that gave them permission not to have babies as teens in Bushwick where they first met. He's on his Apple laptop, a testament to our youth overcoming the digital divide with the confidence in the American dream that *we* gave them even as we were exposing its flaws. She's reading the memoir by Michelle Obama, the First Lady of color and a beautiful dark-skinned woman. Winning has meant a lot of things, not the least of which is having choices. This young couple has an abundance of choices.

The assassinations of Martin Luther King, Jr. and Lil Bobby Hutton galvanized and melded all the factions of the Civil Rights Movement and Black Power movements together because of the ultimate sacrifice that Martin Luther King, Jr. and Lil Bobby Hutton made with their lives. The events of that three day period in April, 1968, showed everybody the naked use of violence and power in the United States. If John F. Kennedy's assassination hadn't done that, then five years later, the double blow of the King and Hutton violent deaths, and then, a few months later, Bobby Kennedy's, revealed that, as H. Rap Brown liked to say then, 'Violence is as American as cherry pie.' It exposed the horribly violent underside to American society. **We won.**

Changing the language and the way black people thought about themselves was the extremely remarkable achievement of the Black Panther Party and of far more value than what the gun did. Jean-Paul Sartre talks about the oppressor, and he says when the oppressed learn the language of the oppressor, then they can use it to tear down the house that is imprisoning them and break the chains. It's not hyperbole to say that the Black Panther Party and the entire civil rights movement saved democracy in 1968. It took 50 years and nine minutes for another martyr, George Floyd, to galvanize another generation to tear down the house and break the chains. **We won.**

I attended a noisy, oh-so-hip rally with Stokely Carmichael at UC Berkeley's Greek Theater on Oct. 29, 1966. Shouting "black power" at the rally was big fun. I was young, one of 14,000 there exercising our right of assembly and free speech. From my parents' living room, I had watched civil rights workers from SNCC, and other Southern organizations in the news, helping people register black people to vote. That situation was very perilous and many died for that. I was entranced by SNCC and, unbeknownst to me or my parents, becoming a radical. As a junior at San Francisco State, I joined the country's first Black Student Union and then, months later with my four roommates, the Black Panther Party. Working on the BPP newspaper and the Breakfast for Children program led to the most harrowing night of my life. King was assassinated on April 4th, 1968, and Lil Bobby Hutton (the BPP's first martyr) on April 6th. The next evening, my fiancé and I came home from planning our wedding to find my apartment had been broken into. Inside were Bobby Seale, Elsa Knight Thompson and Alex, a white radical couple, and two of my ex-roommates. I was 21 and embarrassed because my living room was a mess, dirty laundry all over. Bobby told me to get over it. We began a long run through the night and streets of West Oakland and South Berkeley from safe house to safe house. My roomies quite frankly went through far more on a daily basis on the frontline whereas I was behind-the-scenes editing the BPP paper. But I got caught up in it that night. We heard the police were plotting to take out different Black Panther leaders (police and FBI records document that). There were many urban revolts in the days after Martin Luther King Jr. was killed. There was the possibility that it might happen in Oakland also. The Panthers, through Huey's specific instructions to Bobby disavowing rioting, averted that. My hometown did not go up in flames. **We won.**

I got married in June of 1968, and a year later had a child who became the focus of my life. Five days after I had my son, I finished my B.A. degree, and then five days later, I was offered a teaching job, becoming the youngest faculty member of the nation's first Black Studies department at SF State. Becoming a teacher, mother, and wife was a totally different path. However, I carried many of the ideals and consciousness of the Party into my new roles. But I'm telling you, when I first got in front of classes, even though I had done a lot of tutoring, I realized over and over that I didn't know a damn thing. I had been so busy being an activist I hadn't read enough. That began my lifelong self-learning about history and philosophy, not just of racism and civil rights, but of the world. When I was active in the movement, I was a doer. When I became a teacher, learning and reading became my focus. I wanted to pass on ideas about history and the world through my classes and my writing. **I won.**

Martin Luther King Jr. and Lil Bobby Hutton won. George Floyd won.

Kim, we raised the consciousness of people everywhere. The world changes, moment by moment, war by war, one movement after another. **We won that war.** It's a new day and a new set of wars, backgrounded by that classic era that blossomed into the successes of the feminist movement, ethnic studies movements, disability movement, gray power, brown power, yellow power...one win after another...we won and lived to fight another day.

About the Author

Judy Juanita is an award-winning poet, short story writer, novelist, essayist and playwright. At San Francisco State University in the 1960s, Juanita joined fellow student protesters to revolutionize American higher education and create the nation's first Black Studies department. Juanita was the editor-in-chief of *The Black Panther,* the newspaper of the Black Panther Party. Her semi-autobiographical debut novel, *Virgin Soul* (Viking, 2013), features a young woman in the 1960s who joins the Black Panther Party. Her work is archived at Duke University's John Hope Franklin Research Center, alongside the work of SNCC activists from the 1960s. *De Facto Feminism: Essays Straight Outta Oakland* (EquiDistance, 2016) explores key shifts and contradictions in Juanita's own artistic development as it explores black and female empowerment. She is a winner of the American Book Award (2021) for *Manhattan my ass, you're in Oakland,* a poetry collection. Juanita's twenty-odd plays have been produced in the Bay Area, L.A. and NYC. She appeared in Netflix's *Last Chance U:*Season 5 (2020). Juanita taught at Laney College in Oakland, CA for over three decades. She is a Lecturer in the College Writing Programs at the University of California, Berkeley. In 2024, Juanita received a Reginald Lockett Lifetime Achievement Award from PEN Oakland.